ENTREPRENEURIAL LEADERSHIP AND FINANCIAL STABILITY IN NONPROFIT ORGANIZATIONS

A New Assessment of Social Entrepreneurship and the Social Enterprise

CAROLYN R. MATTOCKS, PhD

abbott press

Copyright © 2017 Carolyn R. Mattocks, PhD.

All rights reserved. No part of this book may be used or reproduced by any means, graphic, electronic, or mechanical, including photocopying, recording, taping or by any information storage retrieval system without the written permission of the author except in the case of brief quotations embodied in critical articles and reviews.

This book is a work of non-fiction. Unless otherwise noted, the author and the publisher make no explicit guarantees as to the accuracy of the information contained in this book and in some cases, names of people and places have been altered to protect their privacy.

Abbott Press books may be ordered through booksellers or by contacting:

Abbott Press
1663 Liberty Drive
Bloomington, IN 47403
www.abbottpress.com
Phone: 1 (866) 697-5310

Because of the dynamic nature of the Internet, any web addresses or links contained in this book may have changed since publication and may no longer be valid. The views expressed in this work are solely those of the author and do not necessarily reflect the views of the publisher, and the publisher hereby disclaims any responsibility for them.

Any people depicted in stock imagery provided by Thinkstock are models, and such images are being used for illustrative purposes only. Certain stock imagery © Thinkstock.

ISBN: 978-1-4582-2152-0 (sc)
ISBN: 978-1-4582-2151-3 (e)

Library of Congress Control Number: 2017918289

Print information available on the last page.

Abbott Press rev. date: 12/12/2017

CONTENTS

ACKNOWLEDGEMENTS

First, I would like to thank God for enabling me to complete the process of writing my dissertation which has expanded into the development of this book. I would like to thank my family for their support, Ronnie, Anniette, Gerald, and Michael as well as all other family members. I would like to thank all institutions of higher learning who played a role in my academic endeavors-North Carolina Central University, North Carolina State University, and Walden University. I would also like to thank Rising Tide Capital, Inc. for allowing me to conduct the study. I appreciate the seven participants who took the time to provide insight about the organization. Without their insight, this study for my dissertation would not have been a success. This book would not be possible. Thank you!!!!!

DEDICATION

This book is dedicated to my parents, Gerald (deceased) and Mae Bell Mattocks who have made sacrifices for me all my life!!!!!

LIST OF TABLES

LIST OF FIGURES

PREFACE

This book uses a case study focusing on the nonprofit organization, Rising Tide Capital, by expanding the scope of Dr. Dees' enterprising nonprofits through an assessment of the meaning of social entrepreneurship, social enterprises, and financial stability. It will also identify financial stability through the two processes of replication (1) replicable models through strategic partnerships and (2) the "mini-franchise" of direct selling for the new and seasoned social entrepreneurs. Below is more detail about the relevance of this case study and the necessity for nonprofits to think about creating enterprising nonprofits for increasing financial stability, but it also enables the new and seasoned social enterprises to think innovatively and creatively about generating consistent cash flow and alternative sources of funding.

Innovation within the financial purview of the nonprofit sector has emerged because of significant budget reductions. Historically, the nonprofit organization has been viewed as a one-dimensional organization solely dependent on grant funding. The current climate of grant funding identifies a need for the social entrepreneur to think about establishing relationships before applying for a grant because of the funders' changing priorities. This change in priorities causes the emerging need for enterprising nonprofits. In 1998, Dr. J. Gregory Dees identified enterprising nonprofits through the social enterprise. The social enterprise is a hybrid structure that enables the nonprofit organization to create a separate entity to generate additional income. Ultimately, Dees concluded that the social enterprise would slow the mission of the nonprofit organization, leaving the social entrepreneur to think about how to create innovative strategies within social entrepreneurship.

Social entrepreneurship using business models can help expand the opportunities for financial stability within nonprofit organizations. The National Council of Nonprofits identified that there are many nonprofits with less than a million dollars in expenditures. Most of these organizations are becoming inactive and there is a need for a leadership style that can embrace business models. Thinking of the nonprofit sector within an entrepreneurial leadership style may identify some of their flaws. A major flaw is revenue diversification. Dees sought to create a solution by highlighting the potential of earning additional income through the social enterprise. The complexities embedded within the social enterprise's structure amplified the relevance of social change value and outcomes. However, the focus of this study was to gain an understanding of how the entrepreneurial leadership style could impact financial stability. The desire to gain an understanding of social entrepreneurship and financial stability led me to finding the Rising Tide Capital nonprofit organization. The organization embraces social entrepreneurship business models that help poverty stricken communities use existing resources to achieve economic empowerment. RTC's ability to diversify their grant funding vehicles provides them with the opportunity to serve more low-income communities. To understand social entrepreneurship, it is necessary to understand the traditional entrepreneurship when linked to financial stability. The umbrella of financial stability causes the nonprofit leader to develop the mindset of a traditional entrepreneur such as passion, resiliency, tenacity, problem solving, creativity, motivation, charisma, and innovation. These are the necessary characteristics to create diversification of revenue and mission sustainability.

This study also provides an overview of the historical foundation of social entrepreneurship and its alignment with social change within various communities. The expansion of social entrepreneurship within the purview of financial stability creates limitations based on the literature about social entrepreneurship and social enterprises. RTC is one of fifteen entrepreneurial nonprofits that embraces social entrepreneurship beyond social change value to maintain their organizations, but an entrepreneurial mindset enables the nonprofit leader to use creativity to identify alternative sources of funding through existing resources that can be replicated.

In this study, the researcher discovered six themes that helps the social entrepreneur create social change and financial stability by applying the mindset of a traditional entrepreneur meaning the use of passion as a strategy to create social benefits and economic stability. Within the study, the researcher could diversify key strategies through replication. RTC functions as a social enterprise without a hybrid structure using replicable models. Their process of replication has crossed seventeen states through strategic partnerships. Replicability was also defined by using the same services and products within the current organizational structure, but using the concept of direct selling meaning a mini-franchise that would function like some of the household names like McDonalds, General Mills, and Kraft. The mini-franchise enables the social entrepreneur to produce alternative source of funding by acquiring an initial investment for each replication of the model and it would create consistent cashflow and prevent the nonprofit organization from being solely dependent on grant funding while increasing revenue diversification.

INTRODUCTION

The National Council of Nonprofits identified that over a million nonprofit organizations ranging from small to mid-size with expenditures of less than $1 million. These organizations are found throughout the country with fewer than 1,000 nonprofits in Wyoming to 40,000 in California. Both the Urban Institute and the Council have demonstrated the deterioration of grant and contract funding. Current issues have focused on the problems of delinquent payments, inadequate indirect and administrative costs, and less than full compensation for the cost of service delivery still plague nonprofits across the nation, but the Council has ideas about resolving these persistent problems.

Nonprofit organizations are the vehicles that provide viable services and solutions to communities by giving them motivation and a source of hope. These organizations turn beliefs into action as promoters of democracy, champions of the common good, incubators of innovation, laboratories of leadership, respondents in times of trouble, stimulators of the economy, and weavers of the community.[1] Starting a nonprofit organization is stimulated by a desire to create change.

Nonprofit organizations embody the dreams and passion of their founders. I can recall the story of Mary McLeod Bethune, who was the founder of Bethune College, which later became Bethune-Cookman College. Bethune started out with a mission to serve underprivileged African Americans within the Daytona Beach, Florida area. With a servant leadership style, Bethune created an institution that has graduated numerous African Americans who carry her legacy out through positions within public, private, and educational sections. However, most of Bethune's funding started out of her pockets as well as the Daytona Beach community.

Current trends of thought about the social enterprise remain like the theories of Dr. J. Gregory Dees with the complexities of how to create a hybrid structure while dealing with the challenges of mission sustainability. The past and current trends of thought have stimulated a new assessment of the social enterprise because of the deterioration of grant funding. The new assessment focuses on the entrepreneurial leadership style that makes the nonprofit organization a fully functioning social enterprise that utilizes their services and products through a process of replication like a private sector entrepreneur while maintaining the sustainability of its mission. In my findings from my research dissertation, I discovered that Rising Tide Capital, Inc. exemplified the characteristics of the new assessment of the social enterprise concept based on the interviews of seven participants which included both the CEO and COO. RTC is one of the few nonprofit organizations that functions as a social enterprise without a hybrid structure.

According to Dees, nonprofits are earning income from third parties to sustain their financial stability.[2] Many nonprofit organizations consider donations and grants as a sign of vulnerability. In the book, *Mission-Based Management: Leading Your Nonprofit Organization in the 21st Century*, by Peter Brinckerhoff, he discussed the need for nonprofit organizations to become financially empowered through seven critical factors. One critical factor is the use of not being dependent on only grant funding, but looking for other types of revenue. According to the article titled, *"Enterprising Nonprofits"* by J. Gregory Dees, an increasing number of nonprofits have been seeking additional revenues by behaving more like for-profit organizations.[3] Dees means that these organizations are becoming more enterprising or entrepreneurial. These organizations are adding more commercialization to their core programs to accomplish their missions. Some are using government contracts, featured work for corporations, and charging beneficiaries for services. Nonprofit organizations are launching business enterprises to sustain their mission. According to a report titled, *"The Sustainability Formula: How Nonprofit Organizations Can Survive in the Emerging Economy,"* one of the most critical factors for creating high performing nonprofit organizations is leadership. The relationship between leadership styles and the financial stability of nonprofit organizations can help nonprofit boards identify leadership styles that have the characteristics of entrepreneurial which help to increase financial stability and restore public trust.

CHAPTER 1

SOCIAL ENTREPRENEURSHIP

Carolyn R. Mattocks, PhD

A Brief Historical Overview of Social Entrepreneurship

The term, entrepreneur, is a French term that dates to the Industrial Revolution.[1] However, there is evidence of entrepreneurship in the early colonial history of the United States. The early colonial traders were considered the most passionate entrepreneurs. These individuals created innovation through trading opportunities and income growth. Emerging from this early success of entrepreneurship was the Industrial Revolution, which was a pivotal period for the American business enterprise.[2] Some early entrepreneurs within the traditional context include Joseph Schumpeter, Andrew Carnegie, John D. Rockefeller, and Adam Smith. These business leaders had tenacity and passion that led to tremendous profits for their businesses. The traditional business enterprise has played a pivotal role in shaping the private sector, which has in turn, transcended into the nonprofit sector. However, the nonprofit sector has had a unique role within the realm of entrepreneurship. The uniqueness comes in the form of social entrepreneurship, which dates to the 18th century, but became more common during the 19th century.

Social Entrepreneurs of the 19th Century

The term, social entrepreneurship, was created by William Drayton, founder of Ashoka.[3] Ashoka was the first organization to provide social entrepreneurship. Drayton received inspiration from Vionda Bhave's Land Gift Movement that aimed at breaking the poverty cycle through a redistribution of land from the rich to the less fortunate.[4] Social entrepreneurs emerged within the 19th century to emphasize the relevance of social change instead of profits. Some of the early pioneers of social entrepreneurship include Robert Owen, Florence Nightingale, and Frederick Olmstead.

Robert Owen: Robert Owen and his conservative movement helped to improve the conditions of factories and factory workers by enabling them to buy goods of sound quality for little more than wholesale cotton and the restriction of the sale of alcohol.[5] Owen was an influential Welsh manufacturer and reformer who became one of the most influential early 19th century advocates of utopian social issues.[6] By 1817, Owen had become a practical reformer because of viable ideas that made him the forerunner of socialism and the cooperative movement. Another aspect of social change that he empowered included the recommendation that villages of "unity and cooperation" be established for the unemployed. Owen also established agricultural communities of between 500 and 3,000 people that would be equipped with the most modern machinery.[7]

Frederick Law Olmstead: Frederick Law Olmstead was an American landscape architect who designed several major public parks such as Central Park in New York City.[8] Olmstead helped with the planning of other sites such as the U.S. Capitol Grounds, the Great White City of the 1893 World's Columbian Exposition, and Boston's Emerald Necklace of Green Space.[9] Olmstead was also the leader of the Yosemite Commission and the campaign to protect Niagara Falls.[10] Olmstead's park and parkway system is registered as a national historic place. Olmstead's method of achieving social change and social entrepreneurship occurred through his passion for architecture. He was the first to think of architecture as a profession. Olmstead espoused the "City Beautiful" movement.[11] This movement aimed at transforming cities with urban policy, such as Rock Creek Park in Jersey City, New Jersey and other park systems in many other cities.[12] Olmstead's motto was that a park is both a work of art and a necessity for urban life. His desire to preserve nature created an "environmental ethic" prior to the environmental movement. Olmstead had a vision to create vast recreational and cultural achievements in the hearts of cities. He saw parks as places of harmony and tranquility. His overarching goal was to advance a feeling of communitiveness, which is a feeling of a shared community and dedicated service to the community among people.

Florence Nightingale: Florence Nightingale was considered the most famous social entrepreneur of the 19th century.[13] She established the first nursing schools and helped to develop modern nursing practices. She was a nurse during the Crimea War in Turkey and became known as the Lady in the Lamp because of her many hours in wards giving care to the wounded.[14] Because of her desire to formalize nursing, she established the first scientifically based nursing school, the Nightingale School of Nursing.[15] She established training for midwives and nurses in workhouse infirmaries.

Social Entrepreneurs of the 20th Century

In the 20th century, social change and social entrepreneurship presented itself through an educator, environmental activist, and the 32nd President of the United States. Each of these individuals upheld a conviction to improve society. The social profits were the number of people that who benefited from the passion of these social change leaders. These social change leaders were relentless to the point where they became fearless when pursuing their mission. The impact of their conviction still has effects on society today. The educational system is still using many of Montessori's methodologies. The environmental movement still learns from the efforts of John Muir. Both the Democratic and Republican parties use the thinking of President Franklin Delano Roosevelt. Each of these individuals exemplified the range of social entrepreneurship and demonstrated the role of social entrepreneurship from both a historical and modern perspective.

Dr. Maria Montessori: Dr. Montessori's social change efforts were critical to the success of early childhood education. Her writings have been translated into different languages such as Japan, China, and Canada. The Montessori method stresses the relevance of respecting children. Most of her studies focused on what were considered convictions that helped her strengthen the process of early childhood education. Some of these philosophical include the following:

- The teacher's role is providing direction and guidance;
- The teacher's role is to help students learn;
- The teacher should present an attitude of love and acceptance in the learning process;
- The teacher's role is to help student reach their fullest potential;
- The teacher is there to create a stimulating learning environment; and
- The teacher is there to ensure the student fulfill their needs.[16]

John Muir: John Muir was an environmental activist, journalist, naturalist, and advocate of the United States Forest Conservation.[17] He founded the Sierra Club for preserving nature. Muir also helped to establish Sequoia and Yosemite National Parks. Whereas his legacy is in environmental activism, the valuable books and articles he produced are lasting imprints of his desire to bring about change.[18] Some of these books include *The Mountains of California (1894), Our National Parks (1901), Stickers: The Story of a Dog (1909), Yosemite (1912) and My First Summer in the Sierra (1911).*

Muir's social change efforts made him a pioneer in the conservation movement. He argued that the Yosemite Valley should become a national park and his efforts influenced President Theodore Roosevelt. Muir's primary conviction was that the wilderness should be federally protected as national parks has given generations of United States citizens an opportunity to appreciate America's landscapes as they exist naturally, in the absence of human industrial influence.[19] The conviction led to the establishment of Mount Rainier National Park in Washington State in 1899 and the Grand Canyon National Park in Arizona in 1919. Muir's writings influence today's naturalists and conservationists. Some of these other writings include posthumous works such as *Travelers in Atlanta (1915), A Thousand Mile Walk (1996), and The Cruise of the Crown: Journal of the Artic Expedition of 1881 in Search of DeLong and the Jeanette (1997).*

Franklin Delano Roosevelt: Franklin Delano Roosevelt was the 32nd president of the United States. Roosevelt became president during the Great Depression and World War II. His social change movements helped to revitalize the America people's faith through programs such as the Tennessee Valley Authority and the New Deal Program.[20] The Tennessee Valley Authority helped to recuperate business and agriculture as well as relief to the unemployed. It also provided to individuals in danger of losing farms and homes.

The New Deal program involved Social Security, heavier taxes on the wealthy, new controls over banks and public utilities, and an enormous work relief programs for the unemployed of the federal government through a series of progress. The New Deal was accomplished during the Roosevelt's first 100 days of office.

Roosevelt's social change legacy began with his leadership as governor. His governorship espoused a progressive government that instituted many new social programs. The presidency of Roosevelt called for quick action that would help to provide economical relief, recovery, and reform. When Roosevelt took office in March 1933, there were 13 million unemployed American and hundreds of banks had closed. The New Deal program had many accomplishments and the most notable include closure of all banks to hold the run on deposits.[21] He also created economic advisors who designed the alphabet agencies such as the Agricultural Adjustment Administration (AAA) to support farm pines, the Civilian Conservation Camps (CCC) to employ young men, and the National Recovery Administration that regulated wages and prices. Roosevelt also established the Good Neighbor Policy with Latin America.

Social Entrepreneurship and Its Alignment with Financial Stability

History has demonstrated the relevance of entrepreneurship and the uniqueness of social entrepreneurship. However, the purview of social and financial stability with the nonprofit motive has been limited. There is an enormous amount of literature about entrepreneurial activity within nonprofit organizations through this concept of social entrepreneurship. The literature also holds examples of a few social enterprises that are like traditional business enterprises. Llewelyn and Kiser discussed social entrepreneurship through a historical and the fields that have been impacted such as health, environment, and enterprise development.[22] According to Llewellyn and Kiser, these social entrepreneurs add an entrepreneurial leadership style to nonprofit organizations, but these enterprises have existed as separate entities that fell under the umbrella of the organization.[23] An example of this would be Cleanslate in Chicago. Carroll, Burke, and Carroll also discussed the use of social entrepreneurship enterprises being embedded within the context of the overarching nonprofit organization to generate additional revenue as well as provide a diversification of funds.[24] Cleanslate is a social enterprise within the CARA Organization that has generated millions of dollars since 2008. The founder used his entrepreneurial skills to attract joint partnerships that helped to increase revenue. However, the entrepreneurial leadership style was not applied to the entire organization. There is some slight evidence that his previous entrepreneurial skills in business helped him with problem solving and branding to make the organization successful.

According to Dees, the spectrum of social enterprises is very broad ranging from commercial to philanthropic.[25] Dees identified a distinct disadvantage of the nonprofit organization is the absence of the profit motive. Profit motive for Dees was finding additional income that would help the organization not be solely dependent on grant funding. According to entrepreneurship theories, it is the entrepreneurial behavior which explains why nonprofit organizations are founded as well as their engagement in provision of services.[26] Kudos used the social enterprise within his discussion to demonstrate how these enterprises obtain funding.[27] These enterprises have the same characteristics as the private sector. The social enterprise model demonstrated how the commercial activities generated various funding streams for the nonprofit organization. Even though the social entrepreneurial leadership style offers an opportunity for the nonprofit to diversify their funding streams, there were some debates if it is a viable solution for financial stability. Initially, there was the debate about the definition of a social enterprise.

According to Trexler, the social enterprise was based on income that is earned for the public's benefit.[28] However, others have defined the social enterprise like a private business. The definition of it being a business have caused the emergence of controversy which identifies the social enterprise as not being a business at all. It is this mindset that continues to have perpetuated a growing concern about the financial planning of nonprofit organizations. The greatest percentage of revenue for nonprofits is funding from grants. Grant guidelines required that the funding be used for the interest of the grantor. The social enterprise has helped the nonprofit diversify their funding streams. There have been examples of many nonprofits relying on funding that they received from a previous grantor. However, if the grantor decides to change their scope, the nonprofit loses a funding source. The entrepreneurial leadership style would force the organization to develop the tenacity to diversify the funding stream like a private business and ultimately not make it dependent on the grants as the only source of income. This approach falls in alignment with underlying principle of a social enterprise perpetuated in Trexler's algorithmic discussion of social enterprises. Trexler states that the "social enterprise reflects a more commercial vision, equating entrepreneurship primarily with earned income.[29] Trexler further identifies the social enterprise as a social business, distinct from mainstream charity in that it eschews grants and donations in favor of financial self-sustainability.[30] Trexler purports that the social enterprise has the capability of closing the gap between the for-profit and nonprofit sectors.[31] He describes this relationship as a hybrid charity/business corporate family such as the Greyston Bakery and the Greyston Foundation. This description of the social enterprise is not a new phenomenon of the entrepreneurial leadership style and its impact on financial stability. The social enterprise is being used as an extension to fulfill the mission. Dees identified the relevance of the social enterprise, but he concluded just like Trexler that it may not be a viable solution. The National Council of Nonprofits' agenda highlights the need for improved leadership and financial stability. The social enterprise is a viable solution, but it would mean moving closer to the traditional theories of entrepreneurship. The traditional theories of entrepreneurship are in alignment with Alexis Tocqueville's landmark description of American voluntarism.[32] This definition describes an array of cooperative enterprises seen at the time as providing a public benefit, many of which we categorize as for-profit business corporations.[33] Embedded with this complexity of the social enterprise is not so much whether it will last, but how best to exhibit corporate life. The way to answer this question that exemplifies this debate about the social enterprise concept structure with the nonprofit is financial stability. It is essential to look at revenue diversification within the nonprofit organizations and then find a way to align it with the entrepreneurial leadership styles and the social enterprise. Carroll and Stater purported that revenue diversification is a viable solution that help to reduce volatility within nonprofit organizations.[34] The revenue diversification would be created through earned income, investments, and contributions. A pertinent question about revenue diversification is whether it would help to increase profitability to the point there would be no resource dependency. Carroll and Stater highlighted that a positive effect is the stability of revenues.[35] However, the goal of revenue diversification is to transcend nonprofit organizations beyond the traditional view which includes charitable donations as their primary source of revenue.[36] Therefore, revenue diversification helps to decrease instability of revenue sources. It is the resource dependency theory that agitates the nonprofit organization, but it also causes support of revenue diversification. It the revenue diversification that sustains the idea that financial decision making is relevant to financial stability. Carroll and Stater identifies that the nonprofit sector has been unique in raising capital, but sustainability has caused the need for revenue diversification which is considered a pivotal revenue generation strategy to alleviate volatility.[37] To achieve revenue diversification, there has been the recommendation of the modern portfolio theory. The modern portfolio theory is based on the principle of risk and return when choosing revenue structures. A concern to draw from revenue generation is the "balancing act" meaning how nonprofit organizations can balance mission and revenue diversification. This is the where the entrepreneurial leadership style would emerge because of the desired to produce profitability. An entrepreneurial leadership style would focus on financial health which includes assets, percentage of revenues, and profitability.

Most nonprofit organizations concern is mission decision. Current theories identify the nonprofit organization decides to implement the social enterprise, it would cause them to lose focus on their mission. Therefore, to sustain profitability, some nonprofits have created hybrid organizations. There is a tendency to use the term nonprofit and social enterprise interchangeably. However, there are distinct differences such as a mission drift. Some believe that the social enterprise would cause the nonprofit organization to lose sight of their mission or impede social value. This has resulted in a hybrid organization better known as the social enterprise which is a combination of both not for profit and the for-profit organization. The hybrid organization has led to the core question of the relevance of the social enterprise. The current literature identifies that there is value and that it should be eliminated from the discussion of the nonprofit sector. However, when you look at the past 30 years and you see the decline in revenue where a less than three fourths of 1% or 21 organizations have grown beyond a budget of $20 million in annual expenditures, then the value of the social enterprise becomes pertinent in the discussion among nonprofit leaders and managers.[38] Therefore, the nonprofit leaders begin to move beyond the resource dependency theory of grants and donations. The focus becomes more about financial sustainability which leads to another core question about how to create mindset that focuses on financial health. In 2052, it is estimated that $6 trillion will flow to social enterprise organizations.[39] This has resulted in emerging opportunities that can help purport the relevance of the social enterprise. The relevance of the social enterprise becomes relevant because of the financial pressures faced by nonprofit organizations. For example, President Bush's budget of 2007-2012 proposed to cut nonprofit funding by $14.3 billion. Research from the Aspen Institute estimates about 20% of nonprofit's revenues comes from private donations including individuals, foundations, and businesses; 30% comes from the state and federal government; while 40% to 50% is earned from service fees.[40] These statistics add more value for the need of the social entrepreneurial leadership style and social enterprise. However, what impedes the success of the entrepreneurial leadership style and social enterprise is that the social entrepreneur's single-minded focus is only on social value. The social entrepreneur utilizes the same mindset of the traditional entrepreneur meaning that he or she seeks capital, but their primary focus is on social benefits and not necessarily financial stability. This lack of focus on the long term identifies why there are financial challenges within the nonprofit sector. These challenges lead back to Brinckerhoff's *Mission-Based Management: Leading Your Nonprofit Organization for the 21st Century* where he establishes that nonprofits must become more financially empowered. To become more financially empowered, the framework of the social enterprise must remove itself from the purview of the hybrid organization. An interesting approach to eliminating the hybrid organization would be the social venture philanthropy concept. In the venture philanthropy model, the donors engage more deeply with the recipient nonprofit organization.[41] This relationship is considered ongoing and the capital is more of an investment rather than a grant. This relationship gains more effectiveness because the social investors also add human capital value through their skills, contacts, credibility, time and personal involvement to the nonprofit. A very good example of the social venture philosophy would be Alfanor which is the first nonprofit organization to use this type of financial model.

Another reason for the need of the social enterprise is the emerging opportunities in financial capital markets. The social enterprise could use these markets because various funds and financial institutions have begun to offer investment opportunities to individuals and institutions that want their resources to both generate social good and provide them with economic return.[42] An example of this would be the Shore Bank Corporation who pioneered this approach in the 1970's. Other recent examples include Triodos Bank of Belgium. The growth of partnerships between philanthropic and commercial leaders also help to strengthen the need for the social enterprise such as the relationship established between the Ford Foundation and the nonprofit, Self-Help, which received a grant of $50 million.

The assessment of the literature demonstrates that there will always be a controversy about the relevance of the social entrepreneurial leadership style, social enterprise, and financial stability. This is related to the early leadership styles of most nonprofit organizations which was servant. However, the social enterprise provides the nonprofit organization with the opportunity to transcend beyond a servant mentality and move into innovation. The innovation has been demonstrated through venture philanthropy and partnerships and more recently evidence-based initiatives with the federal government. The social entrepreneur's mindset must rise above just thinking about social change and social value. Social change can always occur without funding, but the lasting imprint will suffer without a focus on increasing assets, percentage of revenues, and profitability. Experimentation should be eliminated to override the complexities of financial stability, social value and social change.

ENDNOTE

Introduction

1. J.G. Dees, "Enterprising Nonprofits." Harvard Business Review, 1998, 55-67. Carolyn R. Mattocks, "Entrepreneurial Leadership and Financial Stability in Nonprofit Organizations," (PhD diss, Walden University, 2016), 32.
2. J.G. Dees, "Enterprising Nonprofits." Harvard Business Review, 1998, 55-67. Carolyn R. Mattocks, "Entrepreneurial Leadership and Financial Stability in Nonprofit Organizations," (PhD diss, Walden University, 2016), 32.
3. J.G. Dees, "Enterprising Nonprofits." Harvard Business Review, 1998, 55-67. Carolyn R. Mattocks, "Entrepreneurial Leadership and Financial Stability in Nonprofit Organizations," (PhD diss, Walden University, 2016), 32.

Chapter 1: Social Entrepreneurship

1. www.ashoka.org/ashoka&history; Carolyn R. Mattocks, "Entrepreneurial Leadership and Financial Stability in Nonprofit Organizations," (PhD diss, Walden University, 2016), 24.
2. www.ashoka.org/ashoka&history; Carolyn R. Mattocks, "Entrepreneurial Leadership and Financial Stability in Nonprofit Organizations," (PhD diss, Walden University, 2016), 24.
3. www.ashoka.org/ashoka&history; Carolyn R. Mattocks, "Entrepreneurial Leadership and Financial Stability in Nonprofit Organizations," (PhD diss, Walden University,2016), 25.
4. www.ashoka.org/ashoka&history; Carolyn R. Mattocks, "Entrepreneurial Leadership and Financial Stability in Nonprofit Organizations, "(PhD diss, Walden University, 2016), 25.
5. www.britannica.com (Robert Owen); Carolyn R. Mattocks, "Entrepreneurial Leadership and Financial Stability in Nonprofit Organizations," (PhD diss, Walden University, 2016), 25.
6. www.britannica.com (Robert Owen); Carolyn R. Mattocks, "Entrepreneurial Leadership and Financial Stability in Nonprofit Organizations," (PhD diss, Walden University, 2016), 25.
7. www.britannica.com (Robert Owen); Carolyn R. Mattocks, "Entrepreneurial Leadership and Financial Stability in Nonprofit Organizations," (PhD diss, Walden University, 2016), 25-26.

8. www.britannica.com (Frederick Law Olmstead); Carolyn R. Mattocks, "Entrepreneurial Leadership and Financial Stability in Nonprofit Organizations," (PhD diss, Walden University, 2016), 26.

9. www.britannica.com (Frederick Law Olmstead); Carolyn R. Mattocks, "Entrepreneurial Leadership and Financial Stability in Nonprofit Organizations," (PhD diss, Walden University, 2016), 26.

10. www.britannica.com (Frederick Law Olmstead); Carolyn R. Mattocks, "Entrepreneurial Leadership and Financial Stability in Nonprofit Organizations," (PhD diss, Walden University, 2016), 26.

11. www.britannica.com (Frederick Law Olmstead); Carolyn R. Mattocks, "Entrepreneurial Leadership and Financial Stability in Nonprofit Organizations," (PhD diss, Walden University, 2016), 26.

12. www.britannica.com (Frederick Law Olmstead); Carolyn R. Mattocks, "Entrepreneurial Leadership and Financial Stability in Nonprofit Organizations," (PhD diss, Walden University, 2016), 26.

13. www.britannica.com (Florence Nightingale); Carolyn R. Mattocks, "Entrepreneurial Leadership and Financial Stability in Nonprofit Organizations," (PhD diss, Walden University, 2016), 27.

14. www.britannica.com (Florence Nightingale); Carolyn R. Mattocks, "Entrepreneurial Leadership and Financial Stability in Nonprofit Organizations," (PhD diss, Walden University, 2016), 27.

15. www.britannica.com (Florence Nightingale); Carolyn R. Mattocks, "Entrepreneurial Leadership and Financial Stability in Nonprofit Organizations," (PhD diss, Walden University, 2016), 27.

16. www.britannica.com (Dr. Maria Montessori); Carolyn R. Mattocks, "Entrepreneurial Leadership and Financial Stability in Nonprofit Organizations," (PhD diss, Walden University, 2016), 28.

17. www.britannica.com (John Muir); Carolyn R. Mattocks, "Entrepreneurial Leadership and Financial Stability in Nonprofit Organizations," (PhD diss, Walden University, 2016), 28.

18. www.britannica.com (John Muir); Carolyn R. Mattocks, "Entrepreneurial Leadership and Financial Stability in Nonprofit Organizations," (PhD diss, Walden University, 2016), 29.

19. www.britannica.com (John Muir); Carolyn R. Mattocks, "Entrepreneurial Leadership and Financial Stability in Nonprofit Organizations," (PhD diss, Walden University, 2016), 29.

20. www.britannica.com (Franklin Delano Roosevelt); Carolyn R. Mattocks, "Entrepreneurial Leadership and Financial Stability in Nonprofit Organizations," (PhD diss, Walden University, 2016), 30.

21. www.britannica.com (Franklin Delano Roosevelt); Carolyn R. Mattocks, "Entrepreneurial Leadership and Financial Stability in Nonprofit Organizations," (PhD diss, Walden University, 2016), 30.

22. A. Llewelyn, B.W. Jones, & P.M. Kiser, "Social Entrepreneurship," Planning for Higher Education, 2010, p.44-51.; Carolyn R. Mattocks, "Entrepreneurial Leadership and Financial Stability in Nonprofit Organizations," (PhD diss, Walden University, 2016), p.31.

23. A. Llewelyn, B.W. Jones, & P.M. Kiser, "Social Entrepreneurship," Planning for Higher Education, 2010, p.44-51.; Carolyn R. Mattocks, "Entrepreneurial Leadership and Financial Stability in Nonprofit Organizations," (PhD diss, Walden University, 2016), p.31.

24. N. Carroll, M. Burke, and M. Carroll, "A Case of Social Entrepreneurship: Tackling Homeliness, Journal of Business Case Studies, 2010, p. 83-95.; Carolyn R. Mattocks, "Entrepreneurial Leadership and Financial Stability in Nonprofit Organizations," (PhD diss, Walden University, 2016), 31-32.

25. J.G. Dees, "Enterprising Nonprofits." Harvard Business Review, 1998, 55-67. Carolyn R. Mattocks, "Entrepreneurial Leadership and Financial Stability in Nonprofit Organizations," (PhD diss, Walden University, 2016), 32.

26. J.G. Dees, "Enterprising Nonprofits." Harvard Business Review, 1998, 55-67. Carolyn R. Mattocks, "Entrepreneurial Leadership and Financial Stability in Nonprofit Organizations," (PhD diss, Walden University, 2016), 32.

27. J. H. Kudos, Nonprofit Leaders and For-Profit Enterprises. Journal of Entrepreneurship and Public Policy, 2012, p. 147-158.; Carolyn R. Mattocks, "Entrepreneurial Leadership and Financial Stability in Nonprofit Organizations," (PhD diss, Walden University, 2016), 32.

28. J. Trexler. Social Entrepreneurship as An Algorithm: Is Social Enterprise? Complexity and Philosophy, 2008, p. 65-85.; Carolyn R. Mattocks, "Entrepreneurial Leadership and Financial Stability in Nonprofit Organizations," (PhD diss, Walden University, 2016), 33.

29. J. Trexler. Social Entrepreneurship as An Algorithm: Is Social Enterprise? Complexity and Philosophy, 2008, p. 65-85.; Carolyn R. Mattocks, "Entrepreneurial Leadership and Financial Stability in Nonprofit Organizations," (PhD diss, Walden University, 2016), 33.

30. J. Trexler. Social Entrepreneurship as An Algorithm: Is Social Enterprise? Complexity and Philosophy, 2008, p. 65-85.; Carolyn R. Mattocks, "Entrepreneurial Leadership and Financial Stability in Nonprofit Organizations," (PhD diss, Walden University, 2016), 33.

31. J. Trexler. Social Entrepreneurship as An Algorithm: Is Social Enterprise? Complexity and Philosophy, 2008, p. 65-85.; Carolyn R. Mattocks, "Entrepreneurial Leadership and Financial Stability in Nonprofit Organizations," (PhD diss, Walden University, 2016), 33.

32. J. Trexler. Social Entrepreneurship as An Algorithm: Is Social Enterprise? Complexity and Philosophy, 2008, p. 65-85.; Carolyn R. Mattocks, "Entrepreneurial Leadership and Financial Stability in Nonprofit Organizations," (PhD diss, Walden University, 2016), 33.

33. J. Trexler. Social Entrepreneurship as An Algorithm: Is Social Enterprise? Complexity and Philosophy, 2008, p. 65-85.; Carolyn R. Mattocks, "Entrepreneurial Leadership and Financial Stability in Nonprofit Organizations," (PhD diss, Walden University, 2016), 33.

34. D.A. Carroll & K.J. Stater, Revenue Diversification in Nonprofit Organizations: Does It Lead to Financial Stability? Journal of Public Administration Research and Theory, 2008, p.947-966.; Carolyn R. Mattocks, "Entrepreneurial Leadership and Financial Stability in Nonprofit Organizations," (PhD diss, Walden University, 2016), 35.

35. D.A. Carroll & K.J. Stater, Revenue Diversification in Nonprofit Organizations: Does It Lead to Financial Stability? Journal of Public Administration Research and Theory, 2008, p.947-966.; Carolyn R. Mattocks, "Entrepreneurial Leadership and Financial Stability in Nonprofit Organizations," (PhD diss, Walden University, 2016), 35.

36. D.A. Carroll & K.J. Stater, Revenue Diversification in Nonprofit Organizations: Does It Lead to Financial Stability? Journal of Public Administration Research and Theory, 2008, p.947-966.; Carolyn R. Mattocks, "Entrepreneurial Leadership and Financial Stability in Nonprofit Organizations," (PhD diss, Walden University, 2016), 35.

37. D.A. Carroll & K.J. Stater, Revenue Diversification in Nonprofit Organizations: Does It Lead to Financial Stability? Journal of Public Administration Research and Theory, 2008, p.947-966.; Carolyn R. Mattocks, "Entrepreneurial Leadership and Financial Stability in Nonprofit Organizations," (PhD diss, Walden University, 2016), 35.

38. Government Accountability Office, Nonprofit Sector: Significant Federal Funds Reach the Sector Through Various Mechanisms, Report to the Chairman, Committee on the Budget, House of Representatives, 2009.; Carolyn R. Mattocks, "Entrepreneurial Leadership and Financial Stability in Nonprofit Organizations," (PhD diss, Walden University, 2016), 36.

39. V.K. Rangan. The Future of the Social Enterprise. (Working Paper). Harvard Business Review, 2008, p. 2-9.; Carolyn R. Mattocks, "Entrepreneurial Leadership and Financial Stability in Nonprofit Organizations," (PhD diss, Walden University, 2016), 37.

40. www.aspeninstitute.org; Carolyn R. Mattocks, "Entrepreneurial Leadership and Financial Stability in Nonprofit Organizations," (PhD diss, Walden University, 2016), 37.

41. J.W. Skillern, J.E. Austin, H. Leonard, & H. Stevenson. Entrepreneurship in the Social Sector. Los Angeles, CA: Sage Publications, 2007.; Carolyn R. Mattocks, "Entrepreneurial Leadership and Financial Stability in Nonprofit Organizations," (PhD diss, Walden University, 2016), 37.

42. www.alfanor.org (Alfanor)

43. J.W. Skillern, J.E. Austin, H. Leonard, & H. Stevenson. Entrepreneurship in the Social Sector. Los Angeles, CA: Sage Publications, 2007.; Carolyn R. Mattocks, "Entrepreneurial Leadership and Financial Stability in Nonprofit Organizations," (PhD diss, Walden University, 2016), 38.

CHAPTER 2

THE ENTREPRENEURIAL LEADERSHIP STYLE

Strong leadership helps the mission as well as enables the organization to obtain funding resources. While there are many types of leadership styles, the nonprofit sector seems to still struggle to find leadership styles that can help to sustain their financial stability and mission. The entrepreneurial leadership style seems to be one that can apply to the nonprofit sector, but there are others such as transformational and servant. Bass contended leadership is often regarded as the single most critical factor in the success or failure of institutions.[1] Leadership theory began with great man theories, continued with trait theories, situational theories, personal structured theories, psychoanalytic theories, political theories, humanistic theories, interaction and social learning theories.[2] Leadership styles must be able to interface with many groups, stakeholders, and communities, as well as be able to build consensus and teamwork.

Foels, Driskell, and Salas use previous research to look at paradoxes of different leadership styles.[3] The review of literature focuses on the dimensions of how leadership styles can affect the financial success of nonprofit organizations. The literature highlights the transformational leadership style, but there is not a lot of information related to entrepreneurial leadership styles. Geer, Maher & Cole explore the issue of managing nonprofit organizations through transformational leadership to understand how this would apply to nonprofit accountability.[4] Accountability for them is fiscal accountability, good governance, adherence to mission, and program effectiveness. Stull discussed the role of leadership styles and their effectiveness in resolving problems in their communities as well as the creation of opportunities.[5] Leadership is aligned with creating balance to sustain the mission, but there are no conclusions about its relationship to financial stability.

The National Council of Nonprofit Organizations identified that one of the biggest challenges facing nonprofit organizations is also capacity building. Capacity building refers to activities that improve and enhance a nonprofit's ability to achieve its mission and sustain itself over time.[6]. A major gap in the literature is capacity building that focuses on financial stability through asset turnover, profitability and return on invested capital, liquidity, and solvency, percentage of revenues by service, and percentage of expenses by type. Other gaps in the literature are the identification of successful leadership styles besides such as entrepreneurial.

The Council has identified the necessity for improved leadership. To create high performing organizations, there is a need for stronger and innovative leadership that helps to strengthen the cash flow of the nonprofit sector. Brinckerhoff's *Mission-Based Management: Leading Your Nonprofit Organization for the 21ˢᵗ Century* identified seven strategies for the financial empowerment of nonprofit organizations. However, the strategy of the identification of diversifying the revenue was of interest to me. Creating a nonprofit organization with characteristics like the private sector is an innovative way to change it without losing effectiveness.

*In the book, Mission-Based Management: Leading Your Nonprofit Organization for the 21st Century, he identifies eight financial empowerment strategies. However, in this study, I will only highlight the first seven strategies.

Entrepreneurial leadership means that there are certain characteristics that the leader will possess such as tenacity, passion, vision, and flexibility. There is existing information about social entrepreneurship that has been placed under the purview of social profits. Social profits are the benefits that the organization brings to demonstrate social change within communities through numerous services. Social entrepreneurship is not a new phenomenon, but has become a buzzword that has moved the nonprofit organization from being a one-dimensional servant organization to the development of social enterprises.

Interpretations of Entrepreneurial Leadership Style

Beckman, Steiner, and Wassenal highlighted the role of innovation within the context of entrepreneurship.[7] Entrepreneurship is linked with organizational orientation to demonstrate its relevance through key actors that include management, the board of directors, and staff. Carroll, Burke, and Carroll discussed social entrepreneurship to compare agents of change in their communities.[8] The agents used were the traditional social leaders and social entrepreneurs. Soriano and Galindo highlighted that the traditional context of social entrepreneurship was to compare an understanding of entrepreneurial activity within nonprofit organizations. According to Beckman, Steiner, and Wassenal, the success of the entrepreneurial leadership style is dependent on the motivation of key factors such as management, the board of directors, and staff.[9]

The Entrepreneurial Leadership Style in Action

Rising Tide Capital, Inc. uses the entrepreneurial leadership style to develop partnerships with communities that are poverty stricken and filled with unemployment through the concept of entrepreneurship. RTC has been in existence for 10 years because of passion during the tough and prosperous times. This passion from its inception and the number of entrepreneurs created over the past 10 years. RTC was officially incorporated in May 2006. The passion for this idea meant meeting with clients at kitchen tables and cafes. They used this passion as a strategy by using grassroots marketing to stimulate clients to spread the word of RTC's mission. Most traditional entrepreneurs within the private sector use this same tenacity and passion to develop clientele. It has been demonstrated statistically that the best way to develop clients is through word of mouth.[10] The founders of RTC used this passion strategically to determine a niche market that is needed to develop opportunities. The niche market launched the Community Business Academy (CBA) which is a 12-week course offering with hands on training in business planning and management.[11] In September 2006, the CBA graduated its first 15 entrepreneurs. The process that RTC utilizes at the leadership level has been ingratiated through every level of the organization. Passion at every level of the organization causes each person to use its as strategy and tool for problem solving within their roles and responsibilities. Each person is strategically taking responsibility as a role in the ownership of the details. This definition of passion is not traditional because of the use of the social entrepreneurial leadership style that needs a combination of both inward and outward thinking to help identify opportunities that help to expand the mission of the organization. Passion at every level will strengthen capacity building and other opportunities. This thinking helps to remove some of the flaws that are prevalent within the nonprofit model which causes them not to generate revenue and social change which leads to them ultimately becoming inactive.

Table 1. RTC's Passion and Leadership

1. Passion does not have the traditional definition.
2. Passion in the tough times.
3. Passion in the prosperous times.
4. Ownership of the details.
5. Alignment with the role of the organization.
6. Passion must be demonstrated at the leadership level.
7. Passion and strategy.
8. Passion and problem solving.

Source: Dissertation, Entrepreneurial Leadership and Financial Stability in Nonprofit Organizations

Elements of Effective Leadership

In Maxwell's *The 21 Irrefutable Laws of Leadership: Follow Them and People Will Follow You,* he identified are essential characteristics of leadership is leadership ability. Leadership determines a person's level of effectiveness.[12] Without effective leadership, it limits the capability of the organization to develop influence meaning the ability to build social networks and partnerships.

RTC's leadership ability has core elements that help to strengthen organizational performance and financial stability. Core elements of leadership sustains risk taking, tenacity, resiliency, motivation, trustworthiness, and charisma were used to demonstrate the entrepreneurial leadership style. The Council's trends for 2016 highlight leadership development as pivotal for nonprofit impact.[13] The Council does not identify a leadership style, but emphasizes the relevance of leadership development. The Council focuses on the complexities of nonprofit leader. To create success, leaders need support from funders and key partners. The Grantmakers for Effective Organizations (GEO) has found these key characteristics for effectiveness which include collective leadership of teams within and providing continuous support for growth.[14] RTC's leadership ability enables them to create a strong ecosystem for their entrepreneurs. The leveraging of resources through leadership ability broadens their funding opportunities that help to expand their ecosystem of business financing, market opportunities, mentors, coaches, professional services, and other support.

The power of leadership development supports Senge's *Fifth Discipline* and his belief about the learning organization.[15] The five elements that lay the foundation for the learning organization are personal mastery, mental models, team learning, and system thinking. RTC focuses on system building. An organization that focuses on their system functionalities and can extend their leadership abilities to strengthen their mission and vision. RTC's mission and vision is providing viable solutions by building replicable models that help to motivate and uplift distressed communities.

RTC's Entrepreneurial Leadership Style in Action

RTC utilizes creativity within its leadership style affect social change and value through the concept of entrepreneurship. The creativity results in job creation and a revitalization in areas that are overlooked and categorized as the lower class. The entrepreneurial leadership style demonstrated within RTC is like traditional entrepreneurs in the private sector because it takes the same resiliency and tenacity to develop collaborative relationships internally and externally to strengthen growth and development that leads to new directions and opportunities. Within leadership ability is success dedication. Success dedication is based on the ability to influence which is why RTC is people oriented and client oriented. As an entrepreneur, it is essential that you have a buy-in or commitment from your clientele. RTC has achieved this buy-in and commitment through:

1. Transforming lives by heling individuals create a viable means of economic self-sufficiency that can create jobs and expand opportunities;
2. Leveraging existing resources through collaboration and partnerships with other nonprofits, higher education institutions, corporations, and public agencies; and
3. Putting the needs of entrepreneurs first while remaining committed to building a scalable, replicable, and efficient program models with measurable impact.[16]

RTC's effective leadership style is also related to a distributed leadership styles that occurs both internally and externally. Effective leadership style enables distributed leadership among the staff as well as the clients that are becoming leaders in their communities.

Table 2. RTC's Elements of Leadership

1. Resiliency
2. Problem Solving
3. Value Systems
4. Innovation
5. Creativity
6. System Builder-Infrastructure
7. Tenacity
8. Motivation
9. Charisma
10. Visionary
11. Mission-Oriented
12. New Directions
13. Expertise
14. Risk Taking
15. Collaboration
16. Seamlessness-Lack of Deficiencies
17. People-Oriented
18. Strengthen Growth and Development
19. Lack of focus on skillsets
20. Social networks
21. Active listening for opportunities
22. Assessment of internal and external factors
23. Leverages opportunities
24. Transparency
25. Ability to see opportunities
26. Varying levels of leadership

Source: Dissertation: Entrepreneurial Leadership and Financial Stability in Nonprofit Organizations, 2016

Effective Social Entrepreneurship

Historically, it was the social leaders within communities that became the catalyst for social change and social values in communities. These social leaders became early social entrepreneurs who understood the magnitude of their problem which helped them capture the support of funders and stakeholders. Because their focus was mostly social outcomes, it limited their ability to expand their budgets. As the purview of social entrepreneurship began to adopt business models, the need to assess variables such as social value and programmatic worth became more pivotal. Effective social entrepreneurship has the following elements to help sustain their mission and financial stability.

Table 3. Effective Social Entrepreneurship

1. Social Value and Programmatic Worth
2. Competency related to planning
3. Understanding the magnitude of the problem
4. Value and budgets
5. Creativity
6. Replicable model that widens the vision in other areas
7. Embraces the use of business model
8. Ideas and impact
9. Transformation of social value versus money driven
10. Historical transformation
11. Responsive to need
12. Change and needs

Source: Dissertation: Entrepreneurial Leadership and Financial Stability in Nonprofit Organizations, 2016

Effective Social Entrepreneurship in Action

As the nonprofit organization begins to combine social entrepreneurship with business models, the need to assess variables such as programmatic worth become more pivotal. The RTC annual report identifies social value through theory of change. Their theory of change is like Maslow's hierarchy of needs meaning the goal is to reach self-actualization.[17] RTC's effectiveness as social entrepreneurs is that they have identified the magnitude of the problem which is poverty and unemployment. However, it is their intervention through opportunity, impact, and activities which results in self-sufficiency and resiliency.[18] Maslow's hierarchy of needs focuses on moving beyond psychological effects of poverty and unemployment. Removing these psychological barriers to help them develop the belief and esteem to self-actualize becoming an entrepreneur. This theory of change makes them effective social entrepreneurs who is accomplishing both economic empowerment and social change. The RTC's theory of change exemplifies the effectiveness of social entrepreneurship by creating long term value through its mission of economic empowerment through entrepreneurship is not captured merely by revenue growth and he number of job creation, but rather in the way that self-sufficiency and resilience are prerequisites for thriving families and communities.[19] The community business academy and the business acceleration services of RTC which has several 1,000 entrepreneurs demonstrate social value and programmatic worth. An effective social entrepreneur is also creative in developing competency based initiatives and objectives for strategic planning. Creativity is also used to strengthen avenues of funding to further expand domestically and nationally.

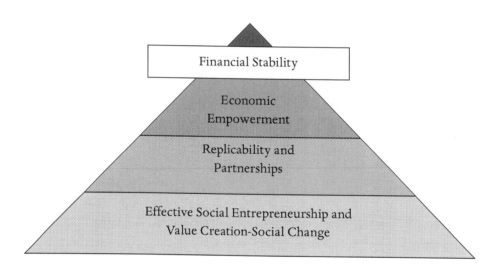

Figure 1: Pyramid demonstrating a hierarchy of needs for the nonprofit organization, Rising Tide Capital, Inc. (Source: Adapted from Maslow's Hierarchy of Needs, Copyright 2016).

ENDNOTE

Chapter 2: The Entrepreneurial Leadership Style

1. B. Bass. The Future of Leadership in Learning Organizations. Journal of Leadership & Organizational Studies, (7)3, 2000, 18-40.
2. B. Bass. The Future of Leadership in Learning Organizations. Journal of Leadership & Organizational Studies, (7)3, 2000, 18-40.
3. R. Foels, et.al. The Effects of Democratic Leadership or Group Members Satisfaction: An Integration. Small Group Research, (31)6, 676-701.
4. B.W. Geer. Managing Nonprofit Organizations: The Importance of Transformational Leadership and Commitment to Operating Standards for Nonprofit Accountability. Performance and Management Review, 32(1), 2008, 51-75.
5. M. Stull. Balancing Market and Mission: A Nonprofit Case Study. Business Renaissance Quarterly. (4)3, 2009, 129-152.
6. www.councilofnonprofits.org (National Council of Nonprofits)
7. A.V. Beckman, S. Steiner, & M.E. Wassenal. Where Innovation Does a World of Good: Entrepreneurial Orientation and Innovative Outcomes in Nonprofit Organizations. Journal of Strategic Innovation and Sustainability, (8)2, 22-36. Carolyn R. Mattocks, "Entrepreneurial Leadership and Financial Stability in Nonprofit Organizations," (PhD diss, Walden University, 2016), 2.
8. N. Carroll, M. Burke, & M. Carroll. A Case of Social Entrepreneurship: Tackling Homelessness. Journal of Business Case Studies, (6)5, 83-95. Carolyn R. Mattocks, "Entrepreneurial Leadership and Financial Stability in Nonprofit Organizations," (PhD diss, Walden University, 2016), 2.
9. A.V. Beckman, S. Steiner, & M.E. Wassenal. Where Innovation Does a World of Good: Entrepreneurial Orientation and Innovative Outcomes in Nonprofit Organization. Journal of Strategic Innovation and Sustainability, (8)2, 22-36. Carolyn R. Mattocks, "Entrepreneurial Leadership and Financial Stability in Nonprofit Organizations," (PhD diss, Walden University, 2016), 2.
10. A. Ries &J. Trout. Positioning: The Battle for Your Mind. New York: NY: McGraw Hill, 2001. Carolyn R. Mattocks, "Entrepreneurial Leadership and Financial Stability in Nonprofit Organizations," (PhD diss, Walden University, 2016), 72.
11. www.risingtidecapital.org (Annual Report); Carolyn R. Mattocks, "Entrepreneurial Leadership and Financial Stability in Nonprofit Organizations," (PhD diss, Walden University, 2016), 72.

12. J. Maxwell. The 21 Irrefutable Laws of Leadership: Follow Them and People Will Follow You. Nashville, TN: Thomas Nelson Company, 1998. Carolyn R. Mattocks, "Entrepreneurial Leadership and Financial Stability in Nonprofit Organizations," (PhD diss, Walden University, 2016), 73.

13. www.councilofnonprofits.org (National Council of Nonprofits); Carolyn R. Mattocks, "Entrepreneurial Leadership and Financial Stability in Nonprofit Organizations," (PhD diss, Walden University, 2016), 74.

14. www.geo.org; Carolyn R. Mattocks, "Entrepreneurial Leadership and Financial Stability in Nonprofit Organizations," (PhD diss, Walden University, 2016), 74.

15. P. Senge. The Fifth Discipline: The Art and Practice of the Learning Organization. New York: NY: Crown, 1994. Carolyn R. Mattocks, "Entrepreneurial Leadership and Financial Stability in Nonprofit Organizations," (PhD diss, Walden University, 2016), 75.

16. www.risingtidecapital.orga (Rising Tide Capital, Inc.). Carolyn R. Mattocks, "Entrepreneurial Leadership and Financial Stability in Nonprofit Organizations," (PhD diss, Walden University, 2016), 75-76.

17. www.pursuit-of-happiness.org (Abraham Maslow); Carolyn R. Mattocks, "Entrepreneurial Leadership and Financial Stability in Nonprofit Organizations," (PhD diss, Walden University, 2016), 83.

18. www.risingtidecapital.org (Rising Tide Capital, Inc.), Carolyn R. Mattocks, "Entrepreneurial Leadership and Financial Stability in Nonprofit Organizations," (PhD diss, Walden University, 2016), 83.

19. www.risingtidecapital.org (Rising Tide Capital, Inc.); Carolyn R. Mattocks, "Entrepreneurial Leadership and Financial Stability in Nonprofit Organizations," (PhD diss, Walden University, 84.

CHAPTER 3

MISSION

Many years ago, nonprofit organizations were viewed as one dimensional organizations that provided very important services to their communities.[1] The National Council of Nonprofits has emphasized the importance of building effective high performing organizations through improved leadership skills.[2] Effective leadership skills help the sustainability of the mission as well as enables the organization to obtain funding sources. To create high performing organizations, there is a need for stronger and innovative leadership that helps to strengthen the cash flow of the nonprofit sector. Brinckerhoff's Mission-Based Management: Leading Your Nonprofit Organization for the 21st Century identified seven strategies for the financial empowerment of nonprofit organizations.[3] However, the strategy of the identification of diversifying the revenue was of interest to me. Creating a nonprofit organization with characteristics like the private sector is an innovative way to change the nonprofit without losing its effectiveness.

The RTC nonprofit was created on the social entrepreneurial concept to strengthen communities and transform lives.[4] It is a 501 (c) 3 tax exempt nonprofit that helps traditionally marginalized population such as women, minorities, and land immigrants transform their lives through entrepreneurship.[5] It is the entrepreneurial spirit that RTC demonstrates through their mission that helps to uplift and motivate distressed communities within Jersey City, New Jersey. The vision of expansion within this entrepreneurial spirit is through the creation of building a replicable model of entrepreneurial development services that can be adopted in other distressed communities to bring about economic empowerment.[6] The excellence that has been demonstrated in this entrepreneurial spirit is based on social change value and outcomes. Values of the organization consist of both people and performance values.

Table 4. People Values

> How we guide our relationship with our clients, team members, funders, board members, and partners.
>
> 1. Honest Communication
> 2. Joyful Productivity
> 3. Mindful Teamwork
> 4. Entrepreneurial Innovation
> 5. Personal Growth and Development
> 6. Commitment to Social Change
> 7. Respect

Source: Rising Tide Capital, 2015

Table 5. Performance Values

> What we demand of ourselves, individually, and as a social enterprise.
>
> 1. Professional Excellence
> 2. Grassroots Methodology
> 3. Quantitative outcomes
> 4. Progress which are:
>   - Efficient
>   - Effective
>   - Sustainable
>   - Salable
>   - Replicable

Source: Rising Tide Capital, 2015

Mission in Action

RTC has two founders, Alfa Demmellash and Alex Forrester. Both are Harvard graduates who have used the social entrepreneurial concept to strengthen and uplift distressed communities in the Jersey City, New Jersey area. The use of a traditional entrepreneur's mindset, which includes both passion and tenacity, has enabled the grant funding structure of RTC to be diverse based on its needs and the requirements of various funders which includes the government, corporate, foundation, and individual philanthropists. A core strategy of RTC is poverty alleviation and economic revitalization. These social value outcomes help support the cliché that if you can teach people to fish, they can motivate and transform their communities; this helps to eradicate poverty. It also teaches people how to successfully create an infrastructure where they are not dependent on a return on investment. RTC is composed of high potential entrepreneurs who help to promote the growth of government programs and it helps them to develop a mindset of self-sufficiency is creating financially independent individuals who are creating strong local economies.[7] This model has received national recognition from former President Barack Obama to the Association for Enterprise Opportunity as a CNN hero.[8] RTC has also received national media exposure on Forbes, Inc.com, Entrepreneurs, Bloomberg Week, and CBS.[9]

The entrepreneurs of RTC can eliminate the mindset of poverty and unemployment to become a productive citizen that offers a sense of hope and inspiration to communities through the concept of entrepreneurship. A storyteller can take her desire to share books and open the mind of kids and give them a sense of belonging. The innovator can create projects that help to increase learning opportunities in his community. The path finder can find self-actualization and overcome the challenge of an unsavory childhood, a troubled marriage, and a few career disappointments. A boot strapper can overcome trauma to provide motivation for women's self-esteem. A role model can uphold the codes of honesty, integrity, and professionalism to achieve 100%

client satisfaction. A pioneer can take his diverse background and transform it into opportunities to help individuals overcome language and cultural barriers. The dream seeker can achieve the American dream through arduous work and open doors to a greater future through her own business. The place maker can transform Whitney Houston's home town into a place of energy with good music and food. These successful entrepreneurs help resolve the problem of poverty and unemployment by transcending these viruses into opportunities of job creation, local economic stimulation and generational wealth.

ENDNOTES

1. www.councilofnonprofits.org (National Council of Nonprofits); Carolyn R. Mattocks, "Entrepreneurial Leadership and Financial Stability," (PhD diss, Walden University, 2016), 1.

2. www.councilofnonprofits.org (National Council of Nonprofits); Carolyn R. Mattocks, "Entrepreneurial Leadership and Financial Stability," (PhD diss, Walden University, 2016),1.

3. P. Brinckerhoff. Mission-Based Management: Leading Your Nonprofit Organization for the 21st Century. New York: John Wiley & Sons, Inc., 2009. Carolyn R. Mattocks, "Entrepreneurial Leadership and Financial Stability in Nonprofit Organizations," (PhD diss, Walden University, 2016), 3.

4. www.risingtidecapital.org (Rising Tide Capital, Inc.); Carolyn R. Mattocks, "Entrepreneurial Leadership and Financial Stability in Nonprofit Organizations," (PhD diss, Walden University, 2016), 64.

5. www.risingtidecapital.org (Rising Tide Capital, Inc.); Carolyn R. Mattocks, "Entrepreneurial Leadership and Financial Stability in Nonprofit Organizations," (PhD diss, Walden University, 2016), 64.

6. www.risingtidecapital.org (Rising Tide Capital, Inc.); Carolyn R. Mattocks, "Entrepreneurial Leadership and Financial Stability in Nonprofit Organizations," (PhD diss, Walden University, 2016), 64.

7. www.risingtidecapital.org (Rising Tide Capital, Inc.); Carolyn R. Mattocks, "Entrepreneurial Leadership and Financial Stability in Nonprofit Organizations," (PhD diss, Walden University, 2016), 64.

8. www.risingtidecapital.org (Rising Tide Capital, Inc.); Carolyn R. Mattocks, "Entrepreneurial Leadership and Financial Stability in Nonprofit Organizations," (PhD diss, Walden University, 2016), 64.

9. www.risingtidecapital.org (Rising Tide Capital, Inc.); Carolyn R. Mattocks, "Entrepreneurial Leadership and Financial Stability in Nonprofit Organizations," (PhD diss, Walden University, 2016), 64.

CHAPTER 4
FLAWS OF THE NONPROFIT MODEL

A Rising Tide Capital employee identified that the nonprofit model was being flawed because of the limitations that have been placed on its functionalities which has caused the need for benchmarking. The National Council of Nonprofits has identified a creation of best strategies or benchmarking.[1] Benchmarking strategies will enable the nonprofit sector to develop ways to improve some of the policies that guide the mission of most nonprofit organizations. In the past, there were restrictions placed on funding because of restricted guidelines. However, the stringent economic budgets have caused a need for the nonprofit sector to focus on entrepreneurial leadership style that embraces business practices from the private sector. With an entrepreneurial leadership style, there is a need to focus on developing market niches. RTC's market niches are the distressed communities that they serve within the State of New Jersey. Like the traditional private sector entrepreneur, they tested the market to determine a need and benefit to their clients. In their book, *Positioning: The Battle for Your Mind*, Ries & Trout highlight the relevance of positioning which means the first body of thought to come to grips with the problem of community in an overcommunicated society.[2] Positioning is not what the product can do, but is about strategically placing it in the mid of the prospect.[3]

Another flaw of the nonprofit model is exciting a community around an idea emotionally, but strategically lack the capability to manipulate what is already in the mind, to retire the connections that already exists.[4] The entrepreneurial leadership style in the nonprofit sector utilizes this marketing approach that is very common in the public sector. RTC's positioning started with ten first year graduates and expanded to 300 graduates. Their growth increased significantly over five years using the concept of positioning to demonstrate entrepreneurship using opportunities that already existed within their communities. A private sector entrepreneur uses the same principles to create growth.

The nonprofit model has been flawed by the inflexibility of funders which has caused nonprofit leaders to have concerns about general operating costs. According to The Council, funders are becoming more flexible by developing unrestricted dollars for capacity capital which helps to strengthen their financial stability.[5] The capacity capital can be used to strengthen human capital meaning there is the capacity to hire qualified staff who are able to strengthen business processes. Volunteers need training to be effective within an organization. Initially, during the startup years of the organization, they are essential in helping to maintain the organization. However, expertise human capital alleviates training dollars that helps to strengthen the financial stability. Each participant emphasized the importance of receiving grants, but it's the diversification of the funder that helps RTC maintain its mission and vision. RTC receives funding from the corporate sector, privates sector, foundations, sponsorships, and individual donors. A traditional entrepreneur in the private sector initially seeks funding from various sources to stay in the "black." Ultimately, the private sector entrepreneur is dependent on the number of sales as well as profits and losses. The entrepreneurial leadership style within the nonprofit sector is dependent on increasing the number of clients serviced within their communities, but they should ensure that mission, goals, and objectives are being met within the scope of their business plans. The nonprofit sector's profitability is more complex because it is dependent on program surpluses and deficits. It is the definition of profitability that distinguishes the nonprofit entrepreneurial leadership style and the private sector entrepreneur. RTC strengthens its revenue portfolio by increasing the number of entrepreneurs being serviced regionally and nationally. It is the sustainability of the mission that becomes pertinent to the nonprofit entrepreneur because profitability means social value and increased support from funders and partnerships. The private sector entrepreneur has more flexibility with their mission and vision because they are seeking to increase customers and sales.

The lack of financial trends is another flaw of the nonprofit model. The nonprofit sector is limited in financial analysis because of a lack of financial schools. Financial trends are very complex within the nonprofit sector because most nonprofit organizations receive funding that will cover at least three years. If they can provide the appropriate quantitative metrics, they can be considered for funding unless the funder changes guidelines. However, when there are economic constraints, most nonprofits may not receive funding. It is the lack of knowledge about financial trends that may agitate the nonprofit sector. A finance manager or budget officer in the nonprofit sector is not concerned about contingency funds. Contingency funds are needed when revenue has become stable or low. A solution for the development of contingency funding is to develop relationships with funders who are supportive of unrestricted funding. The most obvious way to develop contingency funding is through assessing business models. The nonprofit entrepreneurial leadership style has flexibility that enables the adoption of business models as strategies.

Table 6. Flaws of the Nonprofit Model

1. Creation of best practices (Benchmarking)
2. Market Niches
3. Financial Trends
4. Partnerships
5. Unique Selling Position
6. Assessment of business operations
7. Use of business models
8. Cost structures
9. Contingency Funds
10. Revenue portfolio

Source: Dissertation, Entrepreneurial Leadership and Financial Stability in Nonprofit Organizations, 2016

ENDNOTES

1. www.councilofnonprofits.org (National Council of Nonprofits); Carolyn R. Mattocks, "Entrepreneurial Leadership and Financial Stability in Nonprofit Organizations," (PhD diss, Walden University, 2016), 78.
1. A. Ries & J. Trout. Positioning: The Battle for Your Mind. New York: McGraw-Hill, 2001. Carolyn R. Mattocks, "Entrepreneurial Leadership and Financial Stability in Nonprofit Organizations," (PhD diss, Walden University, 2016), 79.
2. A. Ries & J. Trout. Positioning: The Battle for Your Mind. New York: McGraw-Hill, 2001. Carolyn R. Mattocks, "Entrepreneurial Leadership and Financial Stability in Nonprofit Organizations," (PhD diss, Walden University, 2016), 79.
3. A. Ries & J. Trout. Positioning: The Battle for Your Mind. New York: McGraw-Hill, 2001. Carolyn R. Mattocks, "Entrepreneurial Leadership and Financial Stability in Nonprofit Organizations," (PhD diss, Walden University, 2016), 79.
4. A. Ries & J. Trout. Positioning: The Battle for Your Mind. New York: McGraw-Hill, 2001. Carolyn R. Mattocks, "Entrepreneurial Leadership and Financial Stability in Nonprofit Organizations, "(PhD diss, Walden University, 2016), 79.
5. www.councilofnonprofits.org (National Council of Nonprofits); "Entrepreneurial Leadership and Financial Stability in Nonprofit Organizations," (PhD diss, Walden University, 2016), 80.

CHAPTER 5

ENTERPRISING NONPROFITS

Dr. J. Gregory Dees, the father of social entrepreneurship, highlighted the social enterprise concept in 1998. Dees discussed how the social enterprise could add revenue diversification to the nonprofit. However, Dees concluded that the social enterprise was not the right direction for the nonprofit because it could compromise the mission of the organization. The social enterprise has been described as a hybrid organization. A hybrid organization is a nonprofit structure that has created a social enterprise which focuses on adding additional revenue to the organization. The social enterprise concept is being demonstrated in RTC through sources of revenue such as the Community Business Academy, Business Acceleration Services, and the Replication Model. Each help the organization diversify their revenue without compromising their mission. The CBA is a very intensive course in basic business management and planning where entrepreneurs gain hands on familiarity with fundamental concepts, tools, and skills needed to plan and run a successful business.[1] The Business Acceleration Services offer services to individuals in business or just starting your entrepreneurial path.[2] The foundation of RTC is the power of microbusiness which helps to support the social enterprise concept. Microbusinesses employ only 5 or less people and they help to sustain the economy. According to the Association of Enterprise Opportunity, there are 25.5 million microbusinesses in the United States. RTC has added innovation to the social enterprise concept using entrepreneurial energy that already exists in these local economies. RTC strengthens their clientele by providing them with knowledge, capital, social capital, and access to financial capital.

Assessing what Dees concluded about the social enterprise concept caused an assessment of two crucial factors, leadership style and financial stability.[3] These two factors must be intertwined to preserve the mission of the organization. The entrepreneurial leadership style that helps a nonprofit organization create a social enterprise which impacts social change value, but also creates economic empowerment. The communities that RTC serve have many opportunities. However, it is the positioning that must be used to demonstrate value. The typical entrepreneur within an RTC community comes from poverty and unemployment. However, it is the "shift" in moving the business of income constraint that helps RTC move beyond initial theories about the social enterprise.

The Replication Model

Social Entrepreneurship using business models can help expand opportunities and increase financial stability within nonprofit organizations. The National Council of Nonprofits has highlighted several trends in the nonprofit sector. There has been emphasis by the Council to produce high performing organizations. The Council stated that high performing organizations are based on not only the number of grants awarded, but also leadership effectiveness. The Council identified that there are over a million nonprofits with less than a million dollars in expenditures. Most of these organizations are becoming inactive because of their sole dependency on grant funding. This dependency on grant funding requires the need of a leadership style that can embrace business models has the similarities of the traditional entrepreneurs in the private sector business.

Financial stability is one of the biggest challenges facing the nonprofit sector because there are millions of nonprofit organizations that are becoming inactive because of their inability to increase their revenue, assets, and profitability. In the book, *Mission-Based Management: Leading Your Nonprofit Organization in the 21st Century,* Brinckerhoff identified other ways for nonprofit organizations to become financially empowered besides traditional grant funding.[4] Enterprising nonprofits are launching social enterprises to diversify their revenue streams. The key to sustaining a financially empowered nonprofit organization is strong leadership using entrepreneurship. Because of their mission, nonprofit organizations need funding to provide sufficient services.

Dr. J. Gregory Dees concluded that the social enterprise concept was a distraction to the mission of the nonprofit. He did not assess clearly the element of social values and outcomes. His theory was focused on the social enterprise as a vehicle that could generate additional income, but it could also slow the mission of the organization. RTC has taken each of their services and used them as building blocks of their mission. This was the missing link within Dees theories. If you create a social enterprise within the nonprofit structure, each service must be linked to the mission. RTC's social enterprise has the approach where they start with the individual in the community business academy. This graduate then becomes an entrepreneur and goes through their business acceleration services. The social outcomes and value are demonstrated through business development and business expansion. RTC's social enterprise is feasible without a hybrid structure because every service sustains the mission. Therefore, the entrepreneurial leadership style can impact the financial stability of the nonprofit using the social enterprise. It can help to strengthen their assets, revenues, and percentage of revenues. The statement of financial position, the Independent Audit Report 2013-2014 skews RTC's assets growing and the increased profitability. The traditional definition of profitability is social profits based on the outcomes from servicing the community. However, for this study, profitability for the nonprofit was based strictly on the revenue in comparison to the expenses which helped to determine financial stability for the nonprofit organization. Brinckerhoff substantiates in his core principles that not for profit does not mean no profit because it is good for the mission.[5]

Replicability helps to solidify value creation that sustains why it is necessary for nonprofits to find ways to diversify revenue. One participant, COO, identified the relevance of value creation within RTC. Value creation is a unique selling position that can be used to extend the concept into other distressed communities. One participant, CEO, identified that a pilot test is taking place in Chicago to determine how to develop entrepreneurs. The unique selling position is the same philosophy that traditional entrepreneurs use to build leverage in extending their products in other areas. RTC's value creation is demonstrated in the number of successful entrepreneurs that are setting examples of success such as the path finder, the pioneer, the dream seeker, the story teller, the innovator, the place maker, and he legacy builder. Each of these individuals have been taught how to add value creation to their communities by creating services that help to add economic impact to communities that are often overlooked because of poverty and unemployment. The value creation of creating entrepreneurs helps RTC generates $3.80 in economic impact for every $1.00 invested in its progress." Value creation helps a "new RTC business open every 7 days.[6]

Replication within the nonprofit structure is for helping the nonprofit organization achieve financial stability without losing the effectiveness of its mission. The mindset of a social entrepreneur is like the traditional entrepreneur which means there is tenacity, resiliency, and a passion to sustain the mission. One of the themes within my dissertation was passion and leadership. A social entrepreneur uses passion for strategy and problem solving. Strategies and problem solving are based on S.W.O.T. analysis which helps them to determine strengths and opportunities. The social entrepreneur's strengths can be found in its mission which helps the person establish programs based on the assessment of market niches. These programs need funding for implementation. Initially, the funding will occur out of pocket, donations, fundraising activities and grants. When these sources of revenue are exhausted and assets become sparse, the social entrepreneur will use problem solving skills to sustain its mission by utilizing revenue diversification and other alternative sources of funding. Revenue diversification strategies could be assessing the modern portfolio theory meaning investments or it could mean using the replication model which is a new assessment within the context of enterprising nonprofits.

Table 7. Revenue Diversification

1. Generated through services offered by RTC.
2. Opportunities within the communities.
3. Individual donors.
4. Various extension of services
5. Replication model.
6. Expansion of core programs.
7. Fundraising.
8. Diversification of grant funding.
9. Sponsorships.
10. Other earned income.

Source: Dissertation, Entrepreneurial Leadership and Financial Stability in Nonprofit Organizations, 2016

When using the replication model, the role of the social entrepreneur becomes like a traditional entrepreneur, but they do not lose the effectiveness of being a social leader or social change agent. The nonprofit CEO will use his problem-solving skills to determine the appropriate market niches to replicate the model. In my study, the Rising Tide Capital, Inc. was 95% grant funded through several types of grants. However, one of my seven questions focused on alternative sources of funding. Some participants identified a replicable model. Currently, their website sustains replication by crossing 17 states through partnerships that promote the concept of entrepreneurship. Another question to the participant was if they identified their organization as a social enterprise. Each participant confirmed that they were a social enterprise. A social enterprise has been defined as any venture for public benefits using business motives to earn income. In 1998, Dees discussed the social enterprise, but the structure was hybrid. This structure was viewed as a distraction for the mission. Recently, I taught a class titled, *Entrepreneurial Leadership and Financial Stability in Nonprofit Organizations*. During the course, several participants identified with the role of the hybrid structure within the nonprofit organization. One participant identified that the hybrid structure had not been beneficial financially and that there was a need for more strategic planning. Dees identified that the social enterprise as a hybrid structure could slow the mission, but it did give the nonprofit organization the opportunity to earn additional income through contracts, user fees, and partnerships. However, it was Brinckerhoff who also identified the need to stay focused on the mission.

Table 8. Hybrid Organizations Within the Nonprofit Structure (Social Enterprises)

1. Ecological Factors
2. Innovations

Source: Dissertation: Entrepreneurial Leadership and Financial Stability in Nonprofit Organizations, 2016

A New Assessment of the Social Enterprise Concept Using the "I Can Do Anything" Organization, Inc.

The replication which focuses on a new assessment also identifies the social enterprise without the need for the hybrid structure. The additional income for the nonprofit organization would occur using a structure like a private sector concept known as direct selling with elements of network marketing which sounds improbable within the nonprofit structure because of the role of the social entrepreneur as a social change agent. It is feasible for the nonprofit CEO to utilize the literal context of direct selling by sponsoring individuals who may want to establish their own nonprofit organization. These individuals could be volunteer staff or staff who may have this interest because they want to do more within their individual communities. This approach is easing than utilizing cold markets. Volunteers and staff already understand the mission and scope as well as the products and services. Within the purview of direct sales, this is how networks begin to emerge within the nonprofit sector.

Within this new assessment of the social enterprise, the social entrepreneur could be informal or formal. An informal social entrepreneur could be an individual who is focused on creating social value within a community, school or church by selling the products and services that are being replicated within the nonprofit organization. The formal social entrepreneur is interested in being the CEO of a nonprofit organization. This individual would be sponsored by the headquarters and attain a 501 (c) 3. The social entrepreneur would then promote the same products and services established by the headquarters. The social entrepreneur could still seek to attain grant funding or sponsor another individual as a formal social entrepreneur. The formal social entrepreneur could also use direct sales to find informal social entrepreneurs who would purchase the products and then they could create social change by selling them to a school, church or community. Within this structure of networks, the headquarters' nonprofit CEO has not lost the vision of a social entrepreneur and the meaning of social entrepreneurship. A social entrepreneur is a social leader and social change agent seeking to produce social benefits without losing sight of its mission. This structure sustains the mission, but creates alternative sources of funding which Brinckerhoff's seven financial empowerment strategies which also includes an overarching theme of revenue diversification because it would enable them to use grants, fundraising activities, investments, and this additional revenue from direct sales and elements of network marketing would lead to the following:

1. Revenue being more than expenses for at least seven years;
2. Cash operating revenue for at least three months;
3. Annual operating expenses is funded by endowment (5%); and

4. Contingency funding that support and maintain the mission by developing a rapid response mission reserve.[7]

If the social entrepreneur decides to use the direct sales option to sustain the mission, the individual will need to focus on both modeling and selling products. The success from this type of replication will be based on your recruitment strategies. Recruitment strategies such as social media and radio interviews have proven to be extremely effective. The overarching goal of this option is to create consistent cash flow. Using the information for direct sales and applying it to the "I Can Do Anything" Organization as a social entrepreneur means that the immediate products are books and memberships which enables the organization to recruit both formal and informal social entrepreneurs. The formal social entrepreneur is the individual who is interested in managing their own nonprofit organization. The informal social entrepreneur is the individual who will purchase products and create social change in various communities by selling products. Both types of social entrepreneurs keep the mission of social entrepreneurship which is to create social change value and outcomes. It is important for the social entrepreneur to ensure that all aspects of the IRS are followed appropriately meaning 501 (c) 3 tax exempt status, fillings for the state, and the filing of the appropriate tax forms to ensure good standing with the federal and state levels of government. If the social entrepreneur decides to model the business, you have to make sure that each person that is recruited to model the business understands the meaning of social entrepreneurship and the basics of starting a nonprofit organization. It is important that they understand that this only an alternative source of funding that keeps consistent cash flow, but it does not eliminate the pursuit of traditional funding unless you decide to exclusively use your own money or investors This consistent cash flow can help to eliminate the burden of funding your social enterprise initially and the lack of a track record which is required by most grant funders. It gives the social entrepreneur the opportunity to sustain the mission and develop strategic relationships. This alternative source of funding is not meant to be used forever, but it does provide consistent cash flow until the social entrepreneur develops a track record and strategic partnerships with grant funders. The "mini-franchise" within the nonprofit sector starts with the following:

1. Charge a fee that can be invested back in the business to help with salaries, operating expenses, and mission sustainability.
2. Create several models that generate consistent cash flow.
3. Create your recruits from volunteers, regular staff, board members, friends, and family which are individuals who already understand your mission.
4. Create marketing materials that will help position the nonprofit organization such as a catalog, business cards, recruiting brochure, and a starter kit.
5. Develop strategic relationships.

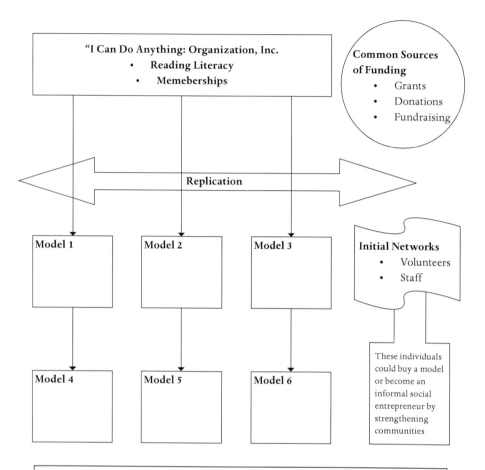

Using the replication model with a direct sales approach with elements of network marketing helps the nonprofit organization achieve financial stability and empowerment. It also sustains the mission and it identifies that a social entrepreneur does not have to function within the hybrid structure. Dr. Dees identified the need for enterprising nonprofits because of his commitment to the meaning of social entrepreneurship and the social entrepreneur. His foundational theories have enabled the new researcher of the social enterprise to sustain the continuous learning, adaptations, and innovation. The new assessment of the social enterprise does not eliminate the hybrid structure. It enables the social entrepreneur to think clearly about strategic planning through the S.W.O.T. analysis. After conducting the S.W.O.T. analysis, the nonprofit CEO will use problem solving, analytical, and critical thinking skills to determine the best approach to creating an enterprising nonprofit organization.

Figure 2: Mini-Franchise, "I Can Do Anything" Organization, Inc.

ENDNOTES

1. www.risingtidecapital.org (Rising Tide Capital); Carolyn R. Mattocks, "Entrepreneurial Leadership and Financial Stability in Nonprofit Organizations," (PhD diss, Walden University, 2016),89.
2. www.risingtidecapital.org (Rising Tide Capital, Inc.); Carolyn R. Mattocks, "Entrepreneurial Leadership and Financial Stability in Nonprofit Organizations," (PhD diss, Walden University, 2016), 87-88.
3. J.G. Dees. Enterprising Nonprofits. Harvard Business Review, 55-67. Carolyn R. Mattocks, "Entrepreneurial Leadership and Financial Stability in Nonprofit Organizations," (PhD diss, Walden University, 2016), 88.
4. P. Brinckerhoff. Mission-Based Management: Leading Your Nonprofit Organization for the 21st Century. New York: John Wiley & Sons, Inc., 2009. Carolyn R. Mattocks, "Entrepreneurial Leadership and Financial Stability in Nonprofit Organizations," (PhD diss, Walden University, 2016), 7.
5. P. Brinckerhoff. Mission-Based Management: Leading Your Nonprofit Organization for the 21st Century. New York: John Wiley & Sons, Inc., 2009.
6. www.risingtidecapital.org (Rising Tide Capital, Inc.); Carolyn R. Mattocks, "Entrepreneurial Leadership and Financial Stability in Nonprofit Organizations," (PhD diss, Walden University, 2016), 86.
7. P. Brinckerhoff. Mission-Based Management: Leading Your Nonprofit Organization for the 21st Century. New York: John Wiley & Sons, Inc., 2009. Carolyn R. Mattocks, "Entrepreneurial Leadership and Financial Stability in Nonprofit Organizations," (PhD diss, Walden University, 2016), 7.

ACTIVITIES

These questions are based on the C-Level of a nonprofit organization meaning the (CEO, COO, CFO). Normally, C-Level analysis is quantitative, but in this document the analysis will be qualitative.

Question 1: Problem Solving as A Nonprofit CEO

As the CEO, your decisions must be concise, integrate detailed analysis in view of the big picture and be action-oriented.

Scenario:

You are the CEO of the nonprofit organization XYZ and you are determining strategies based on a current S.W.O.T. analysis. The S.W.O.T. analysis identified several new opportunities based on an assessment of market niches from the federal, state, and local governments. As well as potentially the private sector. These opportunities were identified because of a weakness from the S.W.O.T. analysis in their last year of funding and that there is a need to prepare for the possibility of a change in the funders' priorities.

Provide an analysis of the following:

1. What have you discovered about the entrepreneurial leadership style when it comes to seeking opportunities within your communities if you do not receive funding?

2. How did you use this leadership style to explore the opportunities in your communities without hurting the mission?

Think about the following:

1. What did you learn #1?
2. What did you learn #2?

Question 2: Critical Thinking

As the CEO, your decisions must be concise, integrate detailed analysis in view of the big picture, and be action-oriented.

Leadership Development in the Nonprofit CEO

Provide the following Analysis:

As a nonprofit CEO, how would you in the initial stages of leadership exposed the elements of leadership in the following areas:

- Creativity
- Passion
- Risk-Taking
- Collaboration
- People-oriented to strengthen growth and development
- Active listening for opportunities
- Assessment of internal and external factors
- Ability to see opportunities
1. What did you learn #1?
2. What did you learn#2?
3. What did you learn#3?
4. What did you learn#4?

Question 3: Analytical

As the CEO, your communications must be concise, integrate detailed analysis in view of the big picture and be action-oriented.

Maxwell identified in his 21 Irrefutable Laws of Success that leadership ability is the key to influencing others. It is a critical factor that can affect the character and morale of the organization. As a nonprofit CEO, you function in a dual role of leadership: leader of the organization and leader of the community.

1. What elements of leadership will be used to strengthen your leadership ability? Why?
2. What have you discovered about leadership ability and its efforts on the success of your organization?

Think about the following:

1. What I learned #1?
2. What I learned #2?
3. What I learned #3?
4. What I learned #4?

Question 4: Financial Analysis

As the CEO, your communications must be concise, integrate detailed analysis in view of the big picture, and be action-oriented.

As the CEO of a nonprofit organization, you are responsible for assessing revenue, cash operating revenue, sources of revenue, and the development of assets. Within the strategic planning process, you fall within the scope of assessing and developing a financial strategic plan. You also would have some oversight of assessing financial challenges that could be problematic within the organization.

1. What would be some ways to strengthen the financial strategic plan?

2. If your nonprofit organization decided that they wanted to use revenue diversification, what would be an approach?
3. What would be your recommendations for alternative sources of funding?
4. Thinking about the seven financial empowerment strategies identified by Brinckerhoff, what would be the areas that the nonprofit organization needs to improve financial stability?

1. What did you learn #1?
2. What did you learn #2?

APPENDIX I

BACKGROUND INFORMATION
(CHAPTER 5, DISSERTATION: ENTREPRENEURIAL LEADERSHIP AND FINANCIAL STABILITY IN NONPROFIT ORGANIZATIONS)

Social entrepreneurship using business models can help expand the opportunities for financial stability within nonprofit organizations. This study focused on the entrepreneurial leadership styles and financial stability in nonprofit organizations. The National Council of Nonprofits has highlighted several trends in the nonprofit sector. There has been an emphasis by the Council to produce high performing organizations. The Council stated that high performing organizations. The Council stated the high performing organizations are based on not only the number of grants awarded, but also leadership effectiveness. In this research study, I identified reasons why the social entrepreneurship leadership style could be used to create social change and financial stability. The National Council of Nonprofits identified that there are over a million nonprofits with less than a million dollars in expenditures. Most of these organizations are becoming inactive because of their sole dependency on grant funding. This dependency on grant funding requires the need of a leadership style that can embrace business models that has similarities of the traditional entrepreneur in the private sector business. Thinking of the nonprofit sector with an entrepreneurial leadership style may identify flaws in the nonprofit sector. A major flaw that was identified was the inability to diversify revenue. Dees sought to create a solution through a social enterprise that would have been an extension to give the nonprofit organization the opportunity to generate additional income. The social enterprise concept created a hybrid structure that led to concerns about the sustainability of the mission of the nonprofit organization. The concept also caused the amplification of the idea that social entrepreneurship focuses on the social change value and social outcomes. However, the focus of the study was to gain an understanding of the entrepreneurial leadership style's impact on financial stability. The desire to gain an understanding of social entrepreneurship and financial stability led me to the Rising Tide Capital nonprofit organization. The organization embraces social entrepreneurship with business models that help poverty stricken communities use existing resources to achieve economic empowerment. RTC's ability to diversify their grant funding from corporate sponsors, foundations, and other grant funding vehicles provides them with the opportunity to serve more low- income communities.

For this research project, I generated data through unstructured, open-ended interview questions with seven participants that worked for RTC. Each participant provided insight about the entrepreneurial leadership style and financial stability in nonprofit organizations. The social entrepreneurial leadership style and social enterprise served as the foundation for the concept and framework for this study. According to the literature, social leaders served as the foundation for stimulating social change and outcomes. Historically, the concept of social entrepreneurship started in the 18th century. The contextual definition of social entrepreneurship emphasizes the relevance of social change instead of profits. In order to understand social entrepreneurship, it is necessary to understand traditional entrepreneurship when linked to financial stability. The umbrella of financial stability causes the nonprofit leader to develop the mindset of a traditional entrepreneur such as passion, resiliency, tenacity, problem solving, creativity, motivation, charisma, and innovation. These are the necessary characteristics to create a diversification of revenue and sustainability of the mission.

This study assessed the historical foundation of social entrepreneurship and its alignment with social change within various communities. However, the expansion of social entrepreneurship into the purview of financial stability created limitations. There was an enormity of literature pertaining to social change entrepreneurship, but not a lot about social enterprises. The social enterprise concept was Gregory Dees, who saw it as an innovative way to generate additional income for the nonprofit. However, Dees ultimately concluded that these enterprises might eradicate the mission of the nonprofit organization. The literature identified the use of social enterprises through Cleanslate within the CARA organization that has generated millions of dollars since 2008. RTC takes a different approach to the social enterprise by stimulating the entrepreneurial spirit within low income communities through ownership of business and job creation. There were other examples within the literature that identified the relevance of social enterprises, but they did not substantiate the social enterprise as a single entity that could sustain its mission as well as maintain financial stability. Brinckerhoff emphasized mission sustainability and financial empowerment. RTC was one of 15 entrepreneurial nonprofits that embrace social entrepreneurship beyond social change value to maintain financial stability. Most nonprofits use grants to sustain their organization, but an entrepreneurial mindset enables the nonprofit leader to gain a commitment and buy-in from finding sources that might not occur if the guidelines are restricted. RTC has been able to survive the challenge of grant funding by expanding stakeholders who can help these identify opportunities beyond just being solely dependent on grant funding.

The six themes that I identified in this study were based on the responses of seven participants. The seven participants included an array of individuals at every level of the organization. The COO of the organization initially identified these individuals during an introductory conversation. The introductory conversation helped to determine the approach for the data collection and data analysis. The data results were credible because I did not have any preconceived biases and was only looking objectively to gain an understanding of the phenomena of the entrepreneurial leadership style and financial stability in the nonprofit sector. I chose to focus on these phenomena because of the development of my own nonprofit organization, "I Can Do Anything." This study required an objectivity that created results that provided solutions about how to use this entrepreneurial leadership style to enhance the strategic planning process as well as begin the process for developing a strategic financial plan. It also enabled me to understand how to apply the social enterprise concept without losing the sustainability of my organization' mission.

The seven participants in this study were comfortable speaking with me and provided valuable insight about RTC. Each participant identified similarities in their responses. Their responses provided insight about the limited properties of the nonprofit sector and bridged the gap of why it is relevant for these organizations to become high performing. It also highlighted the se important trends identified by the National Council of Nonprofits that included improved leadership styles, financial stability, and an emphasis on building greater networks. I identified each of these trends in the responses of the participants which demonstrated the need for the nonprofit sector to expand its scope of thinking and aligning itself with some of the characteristics of the traditional entrepreneur. The use of seven participants did not hurt the credibility of the research. These seven participants enabled me to develop conclusions through data analysis that can add value to the academic and professional communities.

Ashoka. (2015). "What is a social entrepreneur?" Accessed from http://www.ashoka.org/social_entrepreneur

Brinckerhoff, P. Mission-Based Management: Leading Your Nonprofit Organization for the 21st Century. New York: John Wiley & sons, Inc., 2009.

Bryson, J. M. Strategic Planning For Public and Nonprofit Organizations.: A Guide to Strengthening and Sustaining Organizational Achievement. San Francisco: Jossey-Bass, 2011.

Carroll, N., Burke, M. and Carroll, M. "A Case of Social Entrepreneurship: Tackling Homeliness." Journal of Business Case Studies 6, no. 5: 83-95.

Dees, J. G. "Enterprising Nonprofits." Harvard Business Review, 55-67.

National Council of Nonprofits. "Resources." Accessed June 6, 2014, from http:// www.councilofnonprofits.org.

National Council of Nonprofits. "Various Information." Accessed February 14, 2016, from http://www.councilofnonprofits.org.

APPENDIX II

RESEARCH QUESTIONS
(CHAPTER 5, ENTREPRENEURIAL LEADERSHIP AND FINANCIAL STABILITY IN NONPROFIT ORGANIZATIONS)

Central Questions: How does the entrepreneurial leadership style affect the financial stability of Rising Tide Capital and their ability to establish partnerships that help to diversify their assets, profitability, and the percentage of revenues?

Sub-Question 1: How have the assets of Rising Tide Capital grown by using the entrepreneurial leadership style?

Sub-Question 2: Since using the entrepreneurial leadership style, how have assets grown compared to obtaining traditional funding from grants and donations?

Sub-Question 3: How does the entrepreneurial leadership style affect the percentage of revenues within Rising Tide Capital compared to traditional grant funding donations?

The interview protocol had three probing questions and seven other questions to determine the impact of the social entrepreneurial leadership style and affect financial stability.

The first research question focused on the organization as a social enterprise. The goal of my research was to find an organization that functioned in totality as a social enterprise. Based on the literature and Dees, these organizations are hybrid and create volatility for the sustainability of the mission. However, the use of the social enterprise as a single entity such as RTC alleviates the "Jekyll and Hyde" role of the nonprofit leader.

It was the consensus of the seven participants that RTC is a social enterprise. The organization embraces the context of social entrepreneurship with business models that help them create viable solutions for entrepreneurs. These entrepreneurs gain knowledge through their community business academy and business acceleration services. Each of these services help RTC generate financial stability while providing knowledge capital, social capital, and financial capital through existing resources within low income communities to create owners of businesses that stimulate the economy through job creation in communities that are plagued with poverty and unemployment.

The purpose of research question two was to determine the effectiveness of revenue diversification within RTC. Most nonprofit organizations focus only on the mission or on the idea that they can get a grant. The resource dependency theory highlighted the inability of nonprofit organizations to transition beyond grant funding and the restricted guidelines of grant funding. The consensus in the responses of the seven participants identified that RTC is effectively diversifying their revenue. Most of their funding is from a diverse group of funders from corporate, private, and other grant funders. Other funding is through individual donors and other fundraising efforts. The organization also has a focus on creating replicable models that will help them sustain their mission and financial stability. Each participant highlighted the replicable model as a key for effective revenue diversification. Their process of replicability started with a pilot test in Chicago.

Research question three focused on leadership characteristics that would help attract revenue diversification. My goal was to align the mindset of a traditional entrepreneur with the thinking of nonprofit leaders who use the entrepreneurial leadership style. Most nonprofit leaders use a servant leadership style with the focus of providing social benefits and social outcomes to their communities. This results in them becoming social leaders and leads to additional analysis about how to increase revenue.

The consensus of the participants was that RTC has effective leadership. The CEO and COO have the tenacity and resiliency to attract funders who can sustain the passion which leads to innovation and creativity to create opportunities regionally and nationally. The passion can also be used as a strategic tool for problem solving the challenges of financial stability.

Research question four asked if there were similar characteristics of social entrepreneurs and traditional entrepreneurs. As a business owner, the overarching goal is to sustain your business as an organization. Both the social entrepreneur and traditional entrepreneur start with an idea that needs stakeholders to support its sustainability. Without effective leadership ability, that includes the power to influence people, the success of an organization is short-lived with not much social value, social outcomes, or profitability.

The seven participants in this study identified RTC's leadership characteristics as effective. It was the entrepreneurial spirit of meeting in cafes until there was an established site that has given a sense of hope and inspiration to voices of poverty and unemployment to create a viability that did not exist in these communities. The entrepreneurial spirit of passion, tenacity, and resiliency has brought about the social change value of eradicating unemployment to create owners of businesses as well as decrease the unemployment rate through job creation.

I created research question five to explore financial stability in RTC through an assessment of assets, revenue percentages and profitability. Financial stability is not the top priority of most social entrepreneurs, but social benefits, social change value and social outcomes are what motivate them. The social entrepreneur's focus of profitability is only based on social benefits and social value within the communities they serve in their particular state or region.

Each participant identified the need for financial stability. One participant highlighted that within the nonprofit sector, the term profitability is not applicable. He identified that the nonprofit sector focuses on program surpluses and program deficits. During my data collection process, I used the annual report to examine the consolidated financial statements of RTC. Currently, RTC has assets of over 3 million dollars. There is a diversification of revenue. The consolidated statement shows both restricted and unrestricted dollars that can increase capacity building. The entrepreneurial leadership style has transcended RTC beyond traditional grants and donations. RTC receives this type of grant funding, but the replicability concept will increase assets, revenue of percentages, and profitability at the regional and national levels. Even though the focus of social entrepreneurs is the social change value, the current challenges of grant funding causes the social entrepreneur to embraced business models that forces them to develop innovative and creative ways to sustain their mission. RTC has done this through the development of replicable models.

Research question six focused on determining how RTC has used strategic planning and tools through the use of S.W.O.T. helps the organization to appropriately sustain strategic goals and objectives. These strategic goals should include a strategic financial plan that serves as road map to determine trends and how to use current assets to generate other ways to increase revenue and assets. Each participant identified the ways that RTC had diversified their revenue. These ways included grants, individual donations, and the potentiality of replicable models both regionally and nationally. The overall responses provided insight about strategic planning, but not the specificity of a strategic financial plan. The diversification of grant funders helps the organization determine which grants to apply for to support their mission.

Research question seven was asked to identify RTC's plan beyond ten years. Success for a nonprofit's existence is very like a traditional business. If the nonprofit can stay in existence for 5 years, it has the potential for a long-term existence. However, the strategic planning process is essential. The organization has to constantly and consistently identify strengths, weaknesses, opportunities, and threats. The organization has to constantly look for niche markets and identify competitors. The accurate analysis of stakeholders along with the identification of them helps RTC's financial empowerment. The entrepreneurial leadership style is necessary for the financial and economic empowerment of RTC. Each participant identified the ways that RTC has diversified their revenue and that they will become financially empowered. They also believed that the entrepreneurial leadership style will help RTC achieve financial empowerment and economic empowerment. The participants exemplified the relevance of the entrepreneurial leadership spirit is the dream keeper for communities who lose sight of their dreams through no sense of hope and inspiration. However, when they successfully complete the community business academy that gives them knowledge, social and financial capital, then both RTC and each community can achieve economic empowerment. The entrepreneurial leadership style according to the participants makes financial empowerment an achievable goal for RTC.

Dees, J. G. "Enterprising Nonprofits." Harvard Business Review, 55-67.
National Council of Nonprofits. "Various Information." Accessed February 14, 2016, from http://www.councilofnonprofits.org.

APPENDIX III

RECOMMENDATIONS
(CHAPTER 5, ENTREPRENEURIAL LEADERSHIP AND FINANCIAL STABILITY IN NONPROFIT ORGANIZATIONS)

Nonprofit organizations are the vehicles that provide viable services and solutions to communities by giving them the motivation and sense of hope. The RTC mission is to promote an entrepreneurial spirit by demonstrating to its citizens existing resources that can help to create business and jobs. Currently, the RTC nonprofit organization has 3 million dollars in assets based on their consolidated financial statements. According to the National Council of Nonprofits, most nonprofits are becoming inactive because of the deterioration of grants and these organizations also have less than a million dollars in expenditures. For this research project, the goal was to gain an understanding of the entrepreneurial leadership style and financial stability in nonprofit organizations. The findings identified ha this leadership style can help a nonprofit organization gain financial stability. The nonprofit leader has to have similar characteristics as a traditional entrepreneur such as passion, tenacity, problem solving, and resiliency. These characteristics help the nonprofit leader attract opportunities with their existing resources and the proper utilization and identification of stakeholders. The success of the entrepreneurial leadership style and its impact on financial stability within nonprofit organizations leads to further recommendations for research.

A critical aspect of research on this topic would be to further consider the strategic planning process and the use of strategic planning tools to do an accurate analysis of stakeholders, the identification of stakeholders and achieving a commitment and buy-in of stakeholders. This research would help a nonprofit organization lean how to utilize their stakeholders to help them diversify their revenue without losing the sustainability of their mission. Bryson identified in his book, *Strategic Planning*, an array of techniques that could be used to help with the strategic planning process. A technique identified was the stakeholder map. The stakeholder map can help to assess existing stakeholders to identify potential stakeholders for the growth of the nonprofit. RTC has future plans of building replicable models that utilize the current services provided in New Jersey. A strong stakeholder map can help them identify the complexities of using this tool for strategic planning. Leadership style and strategic planning have to be appropriately aligned to achieve financial stability. The National Council of Nonprofits has identified building greater networks as a major trend. This trend established the need for more use of the stakeholder map to create networks through an accurate analysis of stakeholders.

Without the appropriate strategic planning, it becomes difficult for the nonprofit to achieve financial empowerment. An entrepreneurial leadership style that embraces business models can also help to expand the scope of social entrepreneurship. Social entrepreneurship has become a buzzword that is embedded in business schools. It is also beginning to expand into initiatives and institutes at Harvard and Duke. Social entrepreneurship is a concept that needs to be further explored at the international level. RTC's replicable model could be expanded in other countries that could help them continue to achieve financial empowerment. The key for doing this research would be very similar to the pilot test that is being done in Chicago. The CEO could use her native country of Ethiopia to conduct pilot tests to determine if the entrepreneurial model would have the potential at the international level.

Bryson, J. M. Strategic Planning For Public and Nonprofit Organizations.: A Guide to Strengthening and Sustaining Organizational Achievement. San Francisco: Jossey-Bass, 2011.

National Council of Nonprofits. "Various Information." Accessed February 14, 2016, from http://www.councilofnonprofits.org.

APPENDIX IV

CONTRIBUTIONS TO SOCIAL CHANGE
(CHAPTER 5, ENTREPRENEURIAL LEADERSHIP AND FINANCIAL STABILITY IN NONPROFIT ORGANIZATIONS)

The goal of a researcher is to provide vale to the professional and academic communities. It is the idea of the nonprofit that adds social change value and outcomes. However, it is the sustainability of the idea that becomes the challenge for the nonprofit leader. A nonprofit leader can become limited in thinking when it comes to mission sustainability. The focus on mission sustainability allows many leadership styles to fruition the success of providing viable solutions to communities. However, it is the mindset of the entrepreneurial nonprofit leader who uses passion strategically to add social value and strengthen the economy of areas that have the challenges of poverty and unemployment. The entrepreneurial mindset constantly keeps the nonprofit leader aware of the challenges of competitors, the need for the expansion of accurate analysis of the nonprofit leader the opportunity to strengthen areas of the strategic planning process and strategic planning tools. It also enables them to think about opportunities to increase the utilization of their services while sustaining their mission. The opportunities identified through the strategic planning process can help with financial empowerment. The only way for a nonprofit to provide social value is to stay focused on the mission, but have the appropriate strategies to remain financially stable. It is the entrepreneurial mindset that helps the nonprofit thrive financially when there is a deterioration of grant funding.

APPENDIX V

THE BENEFITS OF THIS STUDY TO THE "I CAN DO ANYTHING" ORGANIZATION, INC.

Social change will be demonstrated through my nonprofit organization, "I Can Do Anything." The mission of the organization is to teach youth the importance of starting early learning about career assessments, networking skills, and life skills. Within the strategic planning process, the organization plans to establish partnerships that will them sustain their mission and provide services to youth in grades 8-12. The organization believes that is important for young people to identify their strengths and weaknesses to pave their way to success. Even though this is a solid mission, to bring about social change, I will need to ensure that the organization is financially sound. An entrepreneurial leadership style will help bring about this outcome. I plan to establish partnerships that will diversify revenue and increase assets and plan to establish partnerships that will help to diversify revenue and increase assets and plan to establish partnerships with middle schools, high schools, government agencies, and educational opportunities. I have already become a member of Maryland Nonprofits by contributing to their professional blogs. By doing professional blogging, I could be featured in the spotlight on their webpage. I am also a peer reviewer which helps my organization continue to build stronger relationship with the Maryland Nonprofits. My memberships also helped me learn more about the grants process and how to diversify the organization's portfolio of funding. I also started to build relationships within the Harford County community by joining the Susquehanna Professional Association of Nonprofits (SPAN). I will be able to continue to expose the business which could also lead to other funding opportunities at both the local and state levels. The entrepreneurial leadership style used in the is capacity is almost like the traditional context of entrepreneurship. Most successful entrepreneurs build strong relationships to gain partnerships which helps with the sustainability of their business. With my organization, I am accomplishing social change and profits as well as increasing and diversifying revenue.

APPENDIX VI

DEFINITION OF TERMS
(CHAPTER 1, INTRODUCTION TO THE STUDY, ENTREPRENEURIAL LEADERSHIP AND FINANCIAL STABILITY IN NONPROFIT ORGANIZATIONS)

1. **Entrepreneurship**-A concept that is based on establishing a business entity that will generate a profit.
2. **Hybrid organization**-A hybrid organization is better known as a social enterprise, meaning it functions as a traditional nonprofit with the extension of the social enterprise. **
3. **Modern portfolio theory**-This theory is based on revenue diversification and is a strategy that can be used to show nonprofit organization the importance of investments. ***
4. **Nonprofit organization**-Nonprofits are defined as federally tax-exempt entities to carry out an agency's mission and the relationships are sometimes complex and multi-dimensional. ****
5. **Revenue dependency theory**-A term that has often been associated with nonprofit organizations because of their dependency on grant funding. ***
6. **Revenue diversification**-A term that can be associated with the nonprofit organization by looking at the idea of diversifying earned income through investment portfolios. ***
7. **Revenue generation strategy**-A term that can be associated with the nonprofit sector to help them understand the relevance of diversifying their revenue. ***

8. **Social enterprise**-Any venture that generates earned income for public benefit as well as utilizes efficient business metrics. *****

9. **Social entrepreneur**- A person who is dedicated to strengthening the community by adding social benefits and value. ******

10. **Social entrepreneurship**-A concept that is embedded within the realm of traditional entrepreneurship, but the distinctiveness comes with the desire of the entrepreneur to focus on social change. ******

11. **Great Man Theories**-Great man theory is a 19th century idea according to which history can be largely explained by the impact of "Great Men" or heroes; highly influential individuals who due to either their personal charisma, intelligence, wisdom, or political skill used their power in a way that had a decisive historical impact. *

12. **Social Venture Philanthropy**-This model enables donors to engage more deeply with the recipient nonprofit meaning the relationship is ongoing and the capital is more of an investment rather than a grant. The effectiveness becomes stronger because the social investors also add human capital value theory through their skills, contacts, credibility, and personal involvement to the nonprofit.

13. **Psychoanalytic theory**-The theory of personality organization and the dynamics of personality development that guides psychoanalysis. *

14. **Political theories**-The categorization of social thought by a group or by the persuasion on beliefs of a geo-political mass. *

15. **Trait theory**-An approach the study of human personality based on habitual patterns of behavior, thought, and emotion. *

16. **Situational Theory**-A theory of leadership suggests that no single leadership style is best. This theory is better known Hersey-Blanchard Situational Leadership Theory because of Dr. Paul Hersey, author of the Situational Leader and Ken Blanchard, author of One Minute Manager. *

17. **Personal Structured Theories-**A theory of personality and cognition developed by the American psychologist George Kelly in the 1950s. *

18. **Humanistic Theories-**This theory emphasizes the study of the whole person. *

19. **Interaction Theories-**this theory is an approach to questions about soul cognition, or how one understands other people that focuses on bodily behaviors and environmental contexts rather than mental processes. *

20. **Social Learning Theories-**Bandura's Social Learning Theory posits that people learn from one another, via observation, imitation, and modeling. *

21. **Algorithmic Social Enterprises-**These social enterprises reflect a more commercial vision, equating entrepreneurship primarily with earned income. The social enterprise as a social business distinct from mainstream charity in that it eschews grants and donations in favor of financial self-sustainability.

22. **Transformational Leadership-**These leaders motivates others to do more than originally intended and often even more than possible. They set more challenging expectations and typically achieve higher performance. *

23. **Servant Leadership-**This leadership style is where the leader seeks to serve first and then the leader aspires to lead. *

*These definitions were used from *Leading Organizations* by G.R. Hickman.

** This definition was used from "How Hybrid Nonprofits Can Stay on Mission." Harvard Business School Working Knowledge.

***This definition was used from "Revenue diversification in Nonprofit Organizations: Does It Lead to Financial Stability" by D.A. Carroll & K.J. Stater.

**** This definition was used from "An Investigation of Innovation in Nonprofit Organizations: The Role of Organizational Business." This is from Nonprofit and Voluntary Sector Quarterly.

***** This was used from "Social Entrepreneurship as an Algorithm: Is Social Enterprise Sustainable? by J. Trexler.

****** This was used from "The Meaning of Social Entrepreneurship" by J.G. Dees.

REFERENCES

Alfanor. (2017). Various Information. Accessed August 25, 2017 from http://www.alfanor.org

Ashoka. (2015). "What is a social entrepreneur?" Accessed from http://www.ashoka.org/social_entrepreneur

Aspen Institute (2015). Accessed from June 30, 2015 http://www.aspeninstitute.org

Bahmani,S. Angel, M, & Mendez, M.T. (2013). "Nonprofit Organizations, Entrepreneurship, Social Capital, and Economic Growth. Small Business Economics." Small Business Economics 38, no.3: 271-281.

Beckman, A.V., Steiner, S. and Wassenal, M.E. "Where Innovation Does A World of Good: Entrepreneurial Orientation and Innovative Outcomes in Nonprofit Organizations." Journal of Strategic Innovation and Sustainability 8, no. 2: 22-36.

Bethune-Cookman University. "History." Accessed from http://www.cookman.edu/about_BCU/history/index.html.

Bogdan, R.C. and Biklen, S.K. Qualitative Research for Education: An Introduction to Theory and Methods. Boston: Allyn & Bacon, 1992.

Brinckerhoff, P. Mission-Based Management: Leading Your Nonprofit Organization for the 21st Century. New York: John Wiley & sons, Inc., 2009.

Bryson, J. M. Strategic Planning For Public and Nonprofit Organizations.: A Guide to Strengthening and Sustaining Organizational Achievement. San Francisco: Jossey-Bass, 2011.

Carroll, D.A. and Stater, K.J. "Revenue Diversification In Nonprofit Organizations: Does It Lead to Financial Stability?" Journal of Public Administration Research and Theory 19: 947-966. Accessed, http:/doi: 10.1093/jopart/mun025.

Carroll, N., Burke, M. and Carroll, M. "A Case of Social Entrepreneurship: Tackling Homeliness." Journal of Business Case Studies 6, no. 5: 83-95.

Cheng, V. Case Interview Secrets. Seattle: Innovation Press, 2012.

Creswell, J. W. Qualitative Inquiry and Research Design: Choosing Among Five Approaches. Los Angeles: Sage Publications, 2013.

Creswell, J. W. Research Design: Qualitative, Quantitative, and Mixed Methods Approaches. Thousand Oaks: Sage Publications, 2009.

Dees, J. G. "Enterprising Nonprofits." Harvard Business Review, 55-67.

Dees, J.G. "The Meaning of Social Entrepreneurship." Harvard Business Review, 1-5.

Dal Forno, A. and Merlone, U. "Social Entrepreneurship Effects and the Emergence of Cooperation in Networks." Emergence: Complexity and Organization 11, no. 4:48-58.

Edwards, R. L. and Benefield, E.A.S. Building A Strong Foundation: Fundraising for Nonprofits. Washington, DC: NASW Press, 1997.

Encyclopedia Britannica. "Robert Owen." Accessed from www. britannica.com. .

Encyclopedia Britannica. "Frederick Law Olmstead." Accessed from www.britannica.com.

Encyclopedia Britannica. "Florence Nightingale." Accessed from www. britannica.com.

Encyclopedia Britannica. "Maria Montessori." Accessed from www. britannica.com.

James, N. and Busher, H. "Ethical Issues In Online Educational Research: Protecting Privacy, Establishing Authenticity in Email Interviewing." International Journal of research & Method in Education 30, no. 1: 101-113.

Encyclopedia Britannica. "John Muir." Accessed from www. britannica.com.

Government Accountability Office. Nonprofit Sector: Significant Federal Funds Reach the Sector Through Various Mechanisms, But More Complete and Reliable Funding Data Are Needed. Report to the Chairman, Committee on Budget, House of Representatives, 2009.

Hall, P.D. "A Historical Overview of Philanthropy, Voluntary Associations, and Nonprofit Organizations in the United States, 1600-2000. Harvard Business Review, 1-34.

Harvard Business School Working Knowledge. "How Hybrid Nonprofits Can Stay on Mission. Accessed from http://hbswk.hbs.edu/item/6795.html.

Harvard Business School Business Working Knowledge. "The Growth of the Social Enterprise. Accessed from http://hbswk.hbs.edu/item/3697.html.

Harvard Business School Working Knowledge. "The Coming Transformation of the Social Enterprise." Accessed from http://hbswk.hbs.edu/item/5986.html.

Harvard Business School Working Knowledge. "The Limits of Nonprofit Impact: A Contingency Framework For Measuring Social Performance." Accessed from http://hbswk.hbs.edu./item/6439.html.

Hickman, G.R. Leading Organizations: Perspectives for a New Era. Los Angeles: Sage Publications, 2010.

Kamensky, J. "How Nonprofits and Think Tanks Are Pushing Government to Better Leverage Data. Government Executive, 1-4.

Kudos, J.H. "Nonprofit Leaders and For-Profit Entrepreneurs." Journal of Entrepreneurship and Public Policy 1, no. 2: 147-158.

Kvale, S. and Brinkman, S. Interviews: Learning The Craft of Qualitative Research in Interviewing. Thousand Oaks: Sage Publications, 2009.

Lincoln, Y. S. and Guba, E.G. Naturalistic Inquiry. Beverly Hills: Sage Publications, 1985.

Llewellyn, A. Jones, B.W. and Kiser, P.M. Social Entrepreneurship. Planning for Higher Education 38, no. 4, 44-51.

Mattocks, C.R. Entrepreneurial Leadership and Financial Stability in Nonprofit Organizations. New York: ProQuest, 2016.

Mattocks, C.R. The Use of Successful For-Profit Leadership Styles in the Nonprofit Sector. Walden University, 2012.

Maxwell, J. The 21 Irrefutable Laws of Leadership: Follow Them and People Will Follow You. Nashville: Thomas Nelson Company, 1998.

McDonald, R.E. "An Investigation of Innovation in Nonprofit Organizations: The Role of Organizational Mission." Nonprofit and Voluntary Sector Quarterly 36, no. 2: 256-281. Accessed from http://doi:10.1177/0899764006295996.

Merriam, S. Case Study Research in Education: A Qualitative Approach. San Francisco: Josey Bass, 1988.

Metcalfe, B. A. and Metcalfe, J.A. "The Crucial Role of Leadership in Meeting the Challenges of Change." Journal of Business Perspective 9, no. 2: 27-39. Accessed from http://doi: 10.11771097226290500900205.

National Council of Nonprofits. "Resources." Accessed June 6, 2014, from http:// www.councilofnonprofits.org.

National Council of Nonprofits. "Various Information." Accessed February 14, 2016, from http://www.councilofnonprofits.org.

Pursuit of Happiness. "Abraham Maslow." Accessed from http:// www.pursuito-of-happiness.org/history-of-happiness/ abraham-maslow/.

Research Methods Knowledge Database. "Various Information." Accessed June 29, 2013, from http://www. socialresearchmethods.net/kb/index.php.

Rangan, V.K. "The Future of Social Enterprise." (Working Paper). Harvard Business Review, 2-9.

Ries, A. and Trout, J. Positioning: The Battle For Your Mind. New York: McGraw-Hill, 2001.

Rising Tide Capital. "Various Information." Accessed March 31, 2015, from http://www.risingtidecapital.org.

Rubin, H.J. and Rubin, I.S. Qualitative Interviewing: The Art of Learning Data. Los Angeles: Sage Publications, 2012.

Ryzin, V., Gregg, G. Grossman, S., Stocks, L.D. and Begrud, E. "Portrait of the Social Entrepreneur: Statistical Evidence from a U.S. Panel. Voluntas 20, no. 2: 129-140.

Salamon, L.M. The State of the Nonprofit Sector. Washington, DC: Brookings Institution Press, 2012.

Senge, P. The Fifth Discipline: The Art and Practice of the Learning Organization. New York: Crown, 1994.

Shaw, E. "Marketing in the Social Enterprise Context: Is It Entrepreneurial? Qualitative Market Research 7, no. 3: 194-205.

Skillern, J.W., Austin, J.E., Leonard, H. and Stevenson, H. Entrepreneurship in the Social Sector. Los Angeles: Sage Publications, 2007.

Soriano, D.R. and Galindo, M.A. "An Overview of Entrepreneurial Activity in Nonprofit Organizations in the International Context." Small Business Economy 28: 265-269. Accessed from http://doi.10.1007/s1187-010-9279-2.

Stake, R. The Art of Case Study Research. Thousand Oaks, Sage Publications, 1995.

Stull, M. "Balancing Market and Mission: A Nonprofit Case Study." Business Renaissance Quarterly 4, no. 3: 129-152.

Trexler, J. "Social Entrepreneurship As An Algorithm: Is Social Enterprise Sustainable?" Capacity and Philosophy 10, no. 3: 65-85.

Weinstein, S. The Complete Guide to Fundrasing Management. Hobucken: John Wiley & Sons, 2009.

Yin, R.K. Case Study Research: Design and Method. Thousand Oaks: Sage Publications, 2009.